SKETCH ME, BERTA HUMMEL!

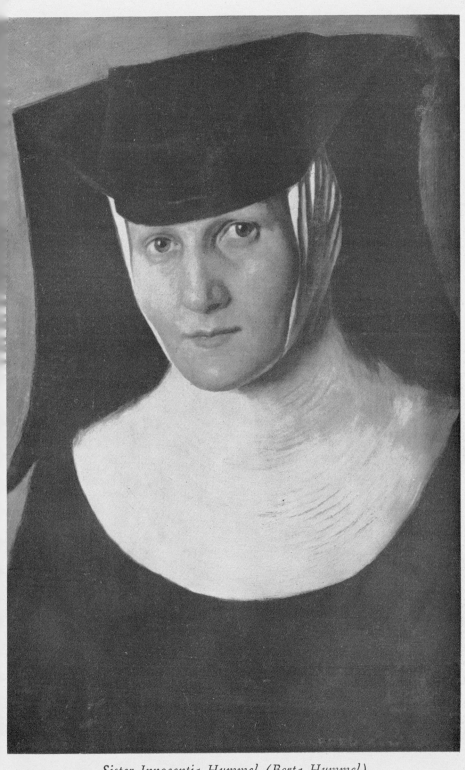

Sister Innocentia Hummel (Berta Hummel)

To Sister Maria Innocentia Hummel

Child of Saint Francis, bearing in thy heart
His creature-love instinct with love of God,
Thou didst seek out the lowly, simple, pure
As fitting best the love theme of thy art.
In canticles Saint Francis sang his joy
In praise of God for sun and humblest grass;
The wayside weed, the bird, the bumble bee
Thy pen and brush did oft employ.
But innocence close cradled in every childish breast,
Kindling the starlight in each pair of guileless eyes,
Innocence, incarnate in Greccio's Babe divine—
This charmed thy palette of its utter best.
To Mary's Child these pages too are given
May they extend in some minutest measure
The mission of thy purity, thy love,
Thy child-like heart.

CHAPTERS

LIST OF PHOTOGRAPHS

Some of the pictures reproduced are done so by the courtesy of Crestwick, Inc. (formerly Ars Sacra), 251 Fourth Avenue, New York 10, New York.

Sketch Me, Berta Hummel!

Biography of Sister Maria Innocentia

(Berta Hummel)

by

Sister M. Gonsalva Wiegand, O.S.F.

GRAIL PUBLICATION

St. Meinrad   Indiana

To All Lovers of the

Hummel Art

AUTHOR'S PREFACE

The definite and widespread interest manifested in the art of Sister Maria Innocentia Hummel, coupled with the lack of any full-length English treatment of her work, has prompted the writing of this biography.

The nature of the existing German works, moreover, and their limited circulation seem to justify this new presentation. DAS HUMMEL BUCH, by Margareta Seeman, for instance, charming in its illustrations and clever interpretative verses, contains little of the artist's biography. HUI, DIE HUMMEL, also largely pictorial, was suppressed during the Nazi regime. Only a few copies of it survive.

The materials for the present work were gathered chiefly by personal correspondence with the Religious Superiors of Sister Maria Innocentia, and her immediate relatives, teachers, and associates.

Grateful acknowledgment is due to Mother Cassiana of the Franciscan Convent at Siessen, to the family of Adolf Hummel, the Sisters of the Holy Family at Munich, the Englischen Fräulein at Simbach, Professor Madame Brauneis, Marga Neises Thomé, Therese Wagner, Martha Goeser and her relatives, and to those who have read the manuscript or have been otherwise instrumental in bringing this work to realization.

A special debt of gratitude is due to my Religious Superiors for their initial permission and subsequent encouragement.

To further, in some small degree, the appreciation of the art of Berta Hummel and so to spread that love of innocence and simplicity which is its theme, is the author's fervent hope.

The Author
Feast of Pentecost, 1949

Chapter One

MASSING

DURING the days preceding the second World War when men presumably should have been enjoying an interim of peace and reconstruction, a great part of the world presented a rather discouraging picture of political adulteration, economic confusion, and systematic corruption of science, education, and morality. Most of the peoples of Europe were laboring in the throes of the impending catastrophe. National leaders were utilizing the efforts and the findings of science only for ulterior and sinister purposes; they sought to conform education and art to their own base standards and distorted ideals, while they used them to implement the tenets of a pragmatic philosophy and an unrighteous morality of their own creation. Nevertheless, in the land where the forces of evil seemed most determined to eradicate all that right-thinking men hold sacred and inviolable, there was at work an opposing force of purity and consecrated service that persistently sought to pierce the gloom and to disperse the miasmic vapors of godlessness and immorality.

Hidden away in a convent in southern Bavaria, a gentle nun was applying talent, time, and energy to reproduce and disseminate the beautiful and the good for the uplifting and enrichment of her fellow countrymen, and ultimately, of the world at large. Her role was not a spectacular one. Undoubtedly her efforts attracted a certain amount of official attention, but what is most remarkable is the fact that her work drew world-wide recognition in spite of its seclusion, its simplicity, and its utter lack of the unusual.

Berta Hummel—in the latter part of her life known in religion as Sister Maria Innocentia—was one of those privileged beings whom an all-kind Providence had enriched with the enviable trait of transforming life's simplest things into the inspiring; the most casual into the profound; the most ordinary into the desired and the acceptable. True to her patronymic "Hummel," which may be interpreted as "Bumble" or "Bee," she possessed the happy faculty of extracting the best, the greatest possible good from that which to others would seem drab and commonplace. Gifted with the double endowment of a fine sense of humor and an unusual artistic ability, she possessed in herself the power to see the bright side of ordinary human affairs and to translate it for the enjoyment and stimulation of her fellowmen. In addition to these gifts of optimism and skill with the brush, this artist-nun was particularly blessed in the wealth of inspiration she received from the scenes and circumstances in which she lived and worked. The products of the Hummel brush and pen, the figurines that have won such popularity, are Berta's interpretation of the colorful, simple life of southern Germany, where she spent her short but prolific life.

The casual visitor to southern Germany is fascinated not only by the grandeur of its rugged scenery, its lofty

2

mountains and wooded hillsides, but also by its pervading religious atmosphere. Just as the massive forests yield place to the peaceful pastures, and the more populous towns alternate with the lowly hamlets, so also the majestic churches of the larger cities have their reflection in the humble rural churches and chapels. Each village cherishes a wayside Calvary, an Olivet, a Madonna, or a shrine to its patron saint. These form the haunts of the lonely, silent worshipper as well as the rallying point of chanting pilgrim groups. The spired church with its gleaming white walls and dark roof is the focal point of the village. From its sanctuary radiates the spirit of fellowship which unites all the families in one great body, sharing common joys and sorrows, and resolving in that wholesome community life that is the distinct mark of the "old-world" German town. Massing, the birthplace of Berta Hummel, is such an ideal spot.

Situated some thirty miles east of Munich and twenty miles north of Oberammergau, Massing shares with the former its rich heritage of art and culture, and with the latter its vast store of medieval lore and pageantry. Thrown into relief by the snow-capped Bavarian Alps in the distant background, this little town of twelve hundred inhabitants may well vie with places of greater pretensions. The sparkling waters of the Rott River thread their way through the valley, reflecting the dark green of the stately pine and fir, mottled with the bright hues of the graceful beech and the sombre foliage of the sturdy oak. As the river passes on its way, the mirrored patches of larch and birch alternate with rich orchards of gold and purple. Couched snugly amid this wooded beauty, Massing, dignified in the symmetry of its Italian architecture, with its gabled roofs of multi-colored tiles, its turrets and moated castle, its vineyards and orchards, presents an attractive picture of peace and contentment.

On an eminence at one end of the town, rearing its lofty spire, stands the parish church of Saint Stephen, about which the farm cottages lie clustered. In an enclosed plot near the church, the villagers have erected as a memorial to honor their war-dead, a majestic monument upon which crouches the figure of a large bear. The names of the fallen heroes are inscribed on a bronze tablet surmounted by a cross. On another eminence at the other end of the town stands the convent of the Poor School Sisters, better known in the United States as the School Sisters of Notre Dame. The convent was originally a castle, the home of the counts of Massing. Its impressive structure adds a medieval touch to the town. Formerly an ancient moat surrounded the castle, but today the convent pond is the only reminder of that symbol of a past age. The center of the town is the residential and business section. Sturdy houses well built of stone and faced with concrete, most of them having two stories and a gable, give a busy and prosperous aspect. Although there are no factories, almost every trade is practiced. The shops form part of the home and usually occupy the portion of the house facing on the street. Here one finds the carpenter and the tailor, the grocer and the baker, the physician and the lawyer, the optician and the jeweler, the wine merchant and the banker, all carrying on a thriving business.

Because of the nature of its activities and the place it holds in relation to the adjoining districts, Massing is known in the local idiom as "Markt Massing." It is a market town, the trade center for the inhabitants of the surrounding countryside and as such it throbs with a certain degree of life and activity. Here the peasants from the nearby farms bring their dairy products and grain, their fruits and vegetables to exchange for cloth and utensils, for an occasional tool or an inexpensive trinket. Such is the daily barter that the little *markt* witnesses, but it reaches its climax periodically when the bustle of a cattle fair stirs the entire countryside.

Berta Hummel has immortalized this scene of her native town in her cartoon "Der Viehmarkt," "The Cattle Fair." With unvarnished realism she portrays the homely prattle and the eager bargaining of scrawny men and buxom women. Nor has she forgotten the children's part in this event. Wide-eyed and open-mouthed, they gape in unfeigned wonder at the hustle and bustle of their elders. In this, as in all her pictures, Berta has caught the atmosphere and the peculiar local idiom of her home town. Its traditions, its unique culture are there.

Margareta Seeman, outstanding German poet and friend of Berta, has enlivened many of the artist's pictures with pertinent verses. She gives an interpretation of "Der Viehmarkt" that defies translation. In quaint Bavarian dialect, she puts into the mouth of the urchin:

> There's something so important
> About a cattle fair,
> There one disputes to heart's content
> Or even explodes with merriment.
> One hears the latest happenings
> Without a penny fee,
> Like when a circus comes to town,
> We children shout with glee.
> Or stand agape with open mouth,
> While mothers have a rest;
> To us such fairs are part of life,
> One every week were best.

But this is only one aspect of the town's mercantile transactions. Business houses of various kinds are located throughout the main portion of Markt Massing. At the end of a busy thoroughfare stands a stately and

5

imposing building two and one-half stories high. A flourishing department store occupies the entire lower part. Its cross-crowned gable, with sculptured Madonna and Child surrounded by angels, suggests a beautiful Italian chapel. Patrons are invited by a carved inscription that reflects the faith of the proprietors:

"Gott gebe jeden der mich kennt, zehnmal so viel als er mir gönnt."

"God reward my patrons tenfold."

Two characteristics of the Firm of J. Hummel are evident from the appearance of this establishment: the economy and consequent prosperity of the proprietors as seen in the attractive window display; and the artistic taste of the residents demonstrated in the exterior sculpture and colorful flower boxes that line the sills of the upper windows. It is no surprise to learn that here is the birthplace and home of Berta Hummel.

This thriving business had been in the Hummel family since 1874. It was the homestead to which Adolf Hummel brought his bride, Victoria Anglsperger, in the spring of 1906. A year later their union was blessed with the arrival of a baby girl, who in holy baptism received the name Katharina. A second daughter, born in 1908, was named after her mother, but soon both children were affectionately called by the household diminutives, Käthi and Viki.

Another year went by and Frau Hummel was looking forward to the birth of her third child. Her husband had been secretly hoping and praying for a male heir, "a fine boy who will help his father in the business." Although he did not realize the fulfillment of that desire, Herr Hummel could never say he was disappointed in the birth of his third child, for on May 21, 1909, a blond, blue-eyed little girl was born to Frau Hummel. Two days later she was baptized Berta.

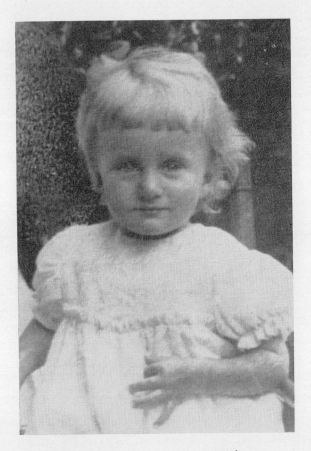

Berta Hummel at two years of age.

Berta Hummel.

Käthi and Viki welcomed the newcomer as a necessary member of their little trio. Viki missed the attentions she had hitherto received which were now of necessity lavished upon the unwitting intruder, but she soon became reconciled and gave unfeigned devotion to her little sister. The atmosphere of love and freedom from care in which the children developed made them strong physically and spiritually. Bertl, as the German diminutive styled her, was especially cheerful in disposition and of such a lively nature that she constantly sought diversion. From her earliest years she manifested a vivid imagination and an artistic temperament. Her spontaneous preference for bright colors, her eagerness to experiment with pencil and scraps of paper were indicative of the latent talent she would soon develop. She would amuse herself for hours in coloring every available picture in newspaper and magazine. It was hazardous to leave ink bottle or paint pot unguarded, for she was sure to utilize its contents. Nevertheless, the chagrin of the elders at the damage done to some precious book or paper would often turn to surprise and amusement when they recognized in the childish scrawl a precocious success in imitating shapes and figures. An appreciation of art and a fair degree of technical skill in this field was a tradition in the family of Adolf Hummel. It was as natural a characteristic as the deep inherent piety of that fine Christian family. Herr Hummel, himself quite a connoisseur, was very proud of the eulogy paid to one of his forbears, Dominic Hummel, a priest who lived from 1769 to 1800:

"The joy of his family, the love of his people, the glory of the priesthood, and of art its charm.... He drew, painted, and sketched beautifully, but nothing more beautiful than the picture of a perfect priest which he sketched by his life."

7

Yes, Adolf Hummel had faith in his daughter's talent for art.

Although Bertl was easily amused by her self-chosen artistic occupations, she was at her best in the midst of a group. Within a few years, the coming of a little brother, Adolf, and of another sister, Crescentia or Cenerl, increased the children's circle to five, so that unselfishness and a willingness to share with others soon became outstanding childhood virtues. The Hummel home was a rendezvous for the neighborhood children. Frau Hummel was glad to have it so. Blessed by God with a large family of her own, she nevertheless was the village Martha who sought to make life happy for all about her. No needy one came to her without receiving help. Even relatives living at a distance preferred to shop at the Hummel store. As adults they recalled the little treats she had arranged for them in their childhood days:

"We children loved to go to the Hummel home. This treat was a rare one, for we lived a distance from the town of Massing. But we always did our shopping there and Mrs. Hummel never failed to put into the package something special for us in the form of a hair ribbon, a handkerchief, or some other trinket that tends to flatter the vanity of little ones."

Frau Hummel exerted great care to instill sound religious and moral training in her children. Before the "Herrgottswinkel" or household shrine, the children recited their daily prayers. Their guardian angel was kept before them as a real companion; the Blessed Virgin Mary was a loving and watchful Mother. By faithfully observing little practices of devotion, the mother carefully trained the children in prayer. At the first stroke of the Angelus bell, she would pause in her work to venerate the sacred mystery of the Incarnation. The children, seeing her, would pause in their play and join their mother in prayer. The family rosary, too, had its place in the Hummel home. While the children were quite young Frau Hummel frequently took them to the village church for services. Quietly and solemnly they would gaze from one picture to another. The beauties of the liturgy and the colorful demonstrations associated with the ceremonies, though not understood by the children, were not lost on their impressionable minds. Berta, particularly, showed great love for the Blessed Sacrament. The organ music delighted her, even as a child of three years.

The pious mother's success in teaching religious truths to the children can be judged from the whole series of religious pictures which Berta sketched in later years. Of these, paintings of the Guardian Angel and of the Madonna are most expressive.

There is a unique appeal in the angel series of the Hummel pictures. With simple but compelling charm Berta presents those homely instances in a child's life that are influenced by its guardian spirit. She shows the protecting power of the angel in the loving solicitude with which he guides the child past the menacing serpent. In another picture the angel is counsellor in encouraging a tearful lad hesitant of a tub of cold water:

"Be brave, my little lad, cold water will not hurt you." Another picture reveals the angel's teaching tactics in the object lesson given an urchin who thoughtlessly dangles a frog by one leg, while the angel in retaliation grasps the forelock of the startled youngster as though he would admonish:

"How would you like such treatment?"

The Madonna pictures are equally expressive. As a child Berta found great delight in providing fresh flowers for the household altar of Our Lady; she was likewise familiar with the wayside shrines that dot the

9

German countryside. She has revived these childhood scenes in her pictures and plastics. One sketch depicts a Madonna before which a five-year-old stands with her little brother. Margareta Seeman's paraphrase of the child's prayer is apt:

Mother Mary, are you weary?
Hand the Baby down to me.
I will hold Him very gently,
And will soothe Him tenderly.
Little Kurt will shoo the insects,
So no harm will come to Him,
And when you are rested, Mother,
We will give Him back again.
In the bush the happy songsters
Make a merry melody,
While for Him the lovely flowers
Cover meadowland and lea.

Berta was but five years old when the roaring of cannon and the marching of troops disturbed the peace and serenity of Massing. On July 23, 1914, war was declared between Austria and Serbia; before many months had passed all the great nations of the earth were to be involved in the First World War. Berta's father was soon called for service in the army and during the coming four years the Hummel household was to be perilously near the fighting at the Austrian border. On September 15, 1914, Franzl, the sixth of the Hummel children, was born.

Life in the household had to go on as normally as possible. Frau Hummel tried to fill the place of both parents to the children; they, in turn, continued their play, their study, and their prayers. Their games were much the same as those of other German children, although for Berta they were frequently supplemented with the artistic touch which her feminine instinct and ingenious skill demanded. Making doll clothes was her favorite pastime, and for this she employed all the art and skill at her command. She made her own patterns and traced her own designs. Although only six years old she showed unusual skill and dexterity. Another loved amusement was pantomiming. In her lively imagination she would people her world with characters from folk and fairy tale, as well as from her own phantasy. She liked to reenact the "Märchen" which her mother, drawing from the rich heritage of German folklore, would tell the children. A shawl, a sheet, a towel might serve for royal robes and fairy garments. Few children of her age could have arranged them with equal skill. When she was at a loss for the necessary stage properties, there was always one member of the household whose wholehearted interest never lagged. This was Lisi, the cook. Lisi knew just what was needed and desired; she could always supply the necessary paraphernalia when everything else failed. Berta knew that faithful Lisi was the mainstay in other ways also. It was she who remembered the birthdays and namesdays and always knew what each one wanted most; it was she who repaired the broken doll, mended the torn frock, planned the parties for which she made good things to eat. Indeed, Lisi was essential in the Hummel household, and certainly she was indispensable for the Hummel shows. Thus Berta's improvised plays were well worth the wild flowers, or pins, or what-nots that order and law demanded for admission into the theatre. There were puppet shows, too, in the Hummel entertainments. Berta usually played the leading role in these juvenile performances, and justifiably, for she had the qualifications of the pseudo-actor: agility, life, expression, and persuasive features. Pleasant reminiscences of these youthful theatricals survive in her portrayals "Die Hexe" and "Hans und Gretel." These pictures prove that the fairy tale was more than a mere story to Berta. Surely, she herself

11

must have had the role of the witch while Cenerl and Ady acted the part of the children.

Twice each year the Hummel family with friends and townsmen made the pilgrimage to Altötting, one of the many places of grace and interest for which Europe, and especially Germany, is famous. This shrine of Our Lady of Mercy attracts hundreds of worshippers from all parts of Europe. Traveling at night, the pilgrims from Massing made the fifteen-mile journey on foot, singing and praying as they went. Most of the adults fasted so that they could receive Holy Communion at the shrine. After the Mass the pilgrims had a period of relaxation and rest, followed by a visit to the many shrines and reliquaries. At sundown they began the trek home.

During the war these religious journeys were more frequent. Berta was only six when she began to accompany her mother and grandfather on these pilgrimages. She was deeply impressed by the image of the black-veiled Virgin and she prayed with all her heart for peace, for her father, and for all who were suffering the hardships of war.

"Dear Mother Mary, you must bring father back to his loved ones, to little Franzl whom he has never seen, to mother who is so often sad and cries so much."

It was while visiting the various shrines and places of interest in Altötting that Berta's grandfather told her of Brother Conrad, the Eternal Porter, who for years had served the pilgrims of Our Lady's shrine. This humble friar had died April 21, 1894, fifteen years before Berta was born, but she was to see in her short lifetime his beatification by Pius XI in 1930, and his canonization four years later. It was from the memories of these pilgrimage stories that she drew her inspiration, when after Brother Conrad was raised to the honors of the altar, she painted a beautiful mural of him for the altar of the parish church at Massing.

12

This picture in the Church of Saint Stephen represents Brother Conrad in the act of distributing bread to the poor. It is among the best of the Hummel paintings.

In this way Berta Hummel, the child-artist, was storing within her young mind the many scenes and experiences of her home town and its environs. Sometimes she was dubbed "Schauerfreitag," the Daydreamer, because of her complete abstraction with some interesting object or creature. The local superstition giving Friday-born children the trait of "Schauen," gazing into the future, was hers by right, since she was born on a Friday. These dreams were not, however, without fruit. Drawings, sketches, cartoons, outlines, were already emerging from her creative hand. Later her proud mother would corroborate this:

"Her first postal cards with personal greetings and sketches made their appearance before Berta was ready for school."

Berta Hummel was always the true child of Massing. She is just as truly the pride of Massing.

Chapter Two

SCHOOL DAYS

BERTA was now six and ready for school. She was about to launch out into a new world—one that held many strange experiences, whose wonders she was anxious to discover and explore. It was the first day of May when she made her initial advance into the new realm of the classroom.

Before 1936 there were two distinct kinds of society in Germany: the classes and the masses. Consequently, there were two separate educational systems to train and equip these groups for their particular place in German society. The Volkschule, or peasants' school, was an eight-year institution giving a thorough foundation in the basic elements of learning. This was followed by a trade training. More than ninety percent of the population attended this type of school.

In sharp contrast to the Volkschule was the system designed for the remaining eight percent, the so-called classes. The elementary school of this institution was followed by a nine-year program, the gymnasium proper. This contrasted sharply with the peasants'

14

Berta Hummel (at right) at the Institute in 1923.

The Graduates at Simbach (Berta—lower middle)

Caricature of her teacher, M. Dasio.

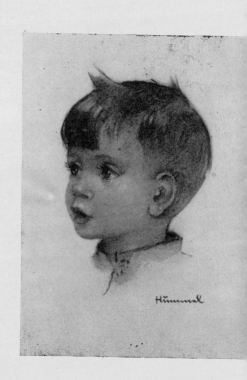

Portrait of Resele Muenck, 1933, Seipen.

At the Cattle Market (See page 5)

Famous Hummel Guardian Angels.

Courtesy of Sacred Art, New York

IX

school in that languages were an integral part of its curriculum. From this school one might advance to the University or professional institutions. In theory, however, the brighter pupils of the Volkschule could transfer to the Collegium, and thus eventually to the University.

Catholic Markt Massing had such a Volkschule; that for the girls was conducted by the School Sisters of Notre Dame in their convent on the hill. Berta was sent to this school for her elementary education. She was eager to go because she had caught some of the enthusiasm of her sisters; her own experiments in school activities had whetted her appetite for learning. Her skillful fingers had imitated the forms of the letters in her picture book. She had sketched her alphabet, had drawn her numbers. There was no doubt that she could easily slip into the routine of the school day which began after the children attended Mass. Reared in the wholesome atmosphere of a God-fearing home, Berta gave her teachers very little trouble. It was easy for the school to build on the foundation so solidly and lovingly laid.

The first two years passed happily enough. Without doubt it was difficult for a child of so lively a disposition to adjust herself to the restriction of the traditional school discipline, but she was docile and obedient and time passed happily. Her teachers commented on her restless ambition and her insatiable curiosity.

During her third year at school, however, a change came over Berta. For one reason or another, school life had changed. A look back into those years reveals the fact that the child was probably suffering from faulty pedagogy. She was in the hands of well-meaning but unsympathetic teachers who very likely could not appreciate her constant restlessness to do, which alternated with her complete engrossment with things beautiful and interesting. Berta was a puzzle to those

15

who did not understand her unusual temperament and for a while this misunderstanding was almost disastrous. Her own mother spoke of this trying year with considerable emotion:

"Gradually we noticed that this child of promise was destined to be a problem child and would cause untold anxiety to loved ones. Her teachers did not understand the temperamental character of their charge. Her usually sunny disposition suffered visibly under the treatment of a teacher who, while well-meaning, was unaware of the psychic condition of the child. When complaints of insubordination reached our home, we attempted to assist the teacher by bringing force and greater vigilance to bear upon a spirit that was already bending under the strain of maladjustment. I can see her yet today, when coming upon her unawares, I caught her in the act of erasing from her slate the report meant for us to censure. Berta trembled visibly when she was discovered, and only then did I realize that her teacher did not understand her. My heart ached for the child and I visited the school pleading that the teacher substitute kindness for severity. Some time later, Berta came to the fourth class. Here a new life began for her. Her teacher knew how to effect a thorough transformation in the child. Her native ingenuity and her sunny disposition were again in evidence. The Sister praised her talents, and yet we never saw her study at home."

The understanding Sister Theresilla knew how to utilize Berta's talents both for the child's artistic development and for her better adjustment at school. In later years this good nun described Berta's progressive attempts to express herself, at first furtively on little scraps of paper, and then gradually in a more overt fashion until she boldly made use of the blackboard.

"What a hubbub of delight prevailed in the class when the little ten-year-old with bold and steady

16

strokes reproduced something pretty, a flower, a gaily colored bird. Her technical skill, her inventiveness and artistic taste enabled her to fascinate her class with charming illustrations. You can imagine with what hilarity a classmate would recognize her own features in the ingenious profile."

With happy wisdom Sister Theresilla appointed Berta to decorate the classroom blackboards for each seasonal celebration. With honest pride the pupils of the fourth class brought parents and friends to enjoy the illustrations in their classroom.

Berta's tricky caricatures at school, as well as her more serious drawings, soon gave her a reputation abroad as her child associates regaled their parents and neighbors with stories of the child-artist's wonderful accomplishments. Had she been more sophisticated her head might have been turned by this admiration, but since lessons and books were rather dull at this time for the little "Hummele," this growing reputation was perhaps a merciful compensation. It gave her, not only a feeling of accomplishment which the natural drive toward success urged her to realize, but it also gave her the satisfaction of knowing that she was making others happy.

"Berta Hummel, sketch me," a playmate would plead.

"Me, too," a chorus would call.

Berta would obligingly comply—even with the demands of those importunate youngsters who intercepted her on the street with orders for a profile. When she had finished her task there were squeals of delight as the fortunate recipient recognized in the crude sketch his own small face. No one was refused; certainly, no one was bored in Berta's company, particularly when she gave vent to her irrepressible tendency to caricature. This skill was developed to an

17

extraordinary degree and was in no wise hindered by
respect for teachers and superiors. What others
might regard as want of proper respect for authority,
she freely accomplished with daring and success. She
would caricature parents and teachers, not secretly and
fearfully, but with a delightful sense of humor, at-
tempting to catch them in an unusual attitude, then
roguishly apprising them of her success.

On the other hand, the child's life had its degree of
shadow caused by the absence of her father. There
were letters from the front, letters eagerly sought and
cherished. For Berta the task of writing to her father meant more than just telling news. She illus-
trated her letters with sketches of herself, of her
mother, her sisters and brothers, and especially of
little Franzl, whom her father had never seen. Berta
drew her stories. Herr Hummel understood and loved
her pictures; he proudly showed them to his "Kamera-
den," the while he prayed for peace and his return to
his family.

"When this is over, Berta will go to the art school,"
he told himself hopefully. "May the end come soon."

Nor was her father the only recipient of Berta's art
beyond the confines of Massing. Parents and friends
of her classmates often asked the little "Hummele" for
sketches of their children and pets. They ordered
postal and greeting cards from her. Many of these,
like Berta's personal ones, found their way to the front
lines.

As in the lives of so many artists and gifted persons
there is exhibited an abnormal urge to productivity, so
in the early life of Berta Hummel while in the Volkschule of the School Sisters at Massing, there is evident the restless genius striving to break its chrysalis
before maturity. It is as though her fervent spirit
sensed the brevity of her young life, and like many of

the saints who crowded mature sanctity into a few years, she accelerated her talent to rich achievement long before its normal development had been attained. The breath-taking output of her early years—largely childish and experimental, it is true—was to continue with little respite throughout her life, even in those last years when her work was unduly curtailed by illness and the cramped conditions in which she was forced to live.

The time was approaching when Berta was to receive her first Holy Communion. With the same whole-heartedness that characterized all her activities, she prepared for the important event. Finally on April 7, 1918, she received her Lord for the first time, from the hands of her pastor, Monsignor Andreas Schonberger, who nine years before had made her a child of God through the holy sacrament of Baptism in this same parish church of Saint Stephen. Berta's most fervent prayer on this great day was for her absent father, "Sweetest Jesus, send my father home and put an end to the war."

Two months later, June 26, 1918, the Bishop of Ratisbon administered the sacrament of Confirmation to the children of Massing. Berta was among those who that day were gloriously charged to be soldiers of Christ. Throughout her life she showed particular awareness of the presence and operation of the Holy Spirit in the Christian soul. Her Pentecostal pictures and other representations of the Holy Spirit are outstanding. In many sketches of the Madonna and Child she includes representations of the Father and the Holy Spirit.

The little "Hummele" was devout, fervent; but she possessed the freedom from care, the spontaneous exuberance that genuine virtue gives to a pure soul. Her disposition had no place for a morbid pietism; neither was she guilty of a giddy irresponsibility, much less of

19

deliberate trouble-making. One who spent her childhood in Massing and knew Berta intimately summed up the happy constituents in her disposition in a few words:

"I can still remember Berta; she was always simple and unassuming. She impressed me especially when in church. Her family had a pew near ours and I could observe her easily. Her recollected attitude, especially during the Elevation, attracted my attention. Others observed her reverent behavior also.

"But she was a gay and lively child—so impetuous— a real "bumble."

Chapter Three

GIRLHOOD

*I*N the ordinary course of human events even the most unusual life can claim only a very small portion as being unique or even different. For the majority of humankind, the life cycle follows a pattern that in many respects is common to every human being. It is a pattern in which the major design is routine, a regular succession of day on day, with one or the other spot highlighted by an occasional important event, an unexpected incident, or an appropriate celebration. This is particularly the case with that period of life between early childhood and adolescence —the time called by some psychologists, childhood proper. It is not that human affairs hold nothing interesting at this period; on the contrary, every event in the least beyond the ordinary is charged with untold secrets and can be made to yield a dynamism wholly unknown, even unguessed by more inhibited minds. For the normal boy and girl, life is a new unfolding thing, and those events that differ from the plan of routine are much more deeply dyed with interest and meaning than most adults usually suppose.

The fact that the early part of her childhood was spent during the years of World War I did make some difference in the life of Berta Hummel, but on the whole, the routine part of her childhood was passed normally enough. During the period that she spent at the Volkschule at Massing her life was shaped by much the same succession of events year after year. These events were somewhat curtailed and modified by the peculiar circumstances through which her country was passing, but by and large, they were the daily and seasonal incidents that were the life of the thriving *markt* in which she lived. Markt Massing, in common with other small communities in Germany, had its own calendar of civic and religious observances that were the very existence of the inhabitants. Since the population was largely Catholic in religious profession and homogeneous in calling and interests, the town's holidays and observances were governed mainly by the feasts of the Church and the exigencies of the season. Everyone in the town, Catholic and otherwise, entered wholeheartedly into these community celebrations either as participants or as spectators.

These festivities were the life of Berta Hummel, the patches of color that brightened the routine of school days and made life meaningful and interesting. Berta had passed her tenth birthday by the time the war had finally ceased and conditions were slipping back into normal. She was now old enough to be able to appreciate the significance of these various seasonal celebrations, to participate in them, and to make her own contribution to their beauty and value. The year 1919-1920 was probably one of the most vital in her early life.

The first event that the postwar lull allowed unhindered observance was the feast of Corpus Christi. The mystery commemorated on this holy day, the abiding Presence of Jesus in the Blessed Sacrament, was

Berta Hummel in her rock garden at twenty-one years old.

IV

The Hummel Home at Massing where Berta was born.

Massing (Upper left at X is the Hummel Home)

dear to the inhabitants of Markt Massing as it is to the heart of every good Christian. The climax of the celebration was the procession of the villagers accompanying the Blessed Sacrament from the church through the streets of the town to the various altars erected at designated places. Here Benediction was given and the Passing Christ was raised to bless the kneeling throngs as He blessed the people of Galilee centuries ago. For the enhancement of this procession the whole village presented the appearance of a gay bazaar, without however, the mirth and confusion of a secular holiday. Homes were decorated and improvised altars were richly ornamented with festoons and candles. The Hummel home, too, was a scene of simple beauty and devotion. Berta had made a triumphal arch bearing the inscription, "Blessed is He Who cometh in the Name of the Lord." On the windowsills, decorated with colorful flower-boxes and candles, stood statues of Our Lady and of Saint Joseph.

Berta herself walked with the school children in the procession. All the girls dressed in white and wore wreaths of flowers in their hair. From a basket hanging from a ribbon about their necks they strewed flowers along the route of the procession. There were others in the escort, for the entire town took part in the event: the societies and confraternities in their distinctive uniforms followed the banner or image of their patron saint; silent altar boys carried candles or swinging censers; and then a motley group of villagers —here an old man leaning on the arms of his grandson, there a young mother, babe in arms and two more holding to her skirts—walked painfully along, telling their beads. Yet they were all united in a community of devotion and religious fervor, in a concerted effort to honor their Lord and God. In later years Berta commemorated this event in her Corpus Christi picture which depicts two children singing and strewing flowers. She has given to these two youthful worshippers the charm and innocence, the reverent faith and trust that are so natural to childhood.

Perhaps of even more attraction to Berta than the Corpus Christi celebration was the observance of Advent and its sequel, Christmas. It was probably another year, the winter of 1920, when this season could be observed with all its old-time custom. It was ushered in with the hanging of the Advent wreath. In accord with the custom observed in most Bavarian homes, the Hummels had their Advent wreath of evergreen. It was suspended horizontally above the dining room table and four candles, fastened equally distant from each other, projected upward from it. These candles were symbolic of the four Sundays of Advent which in turn typify the four thousand years of waiting before the coming of Christ. On the first Sunday of Advent Herr Hummel as head of the household lighted the first candle which burnt thereafter during the meals. The following Saturday it was Frau Hummel's turn to light the second candle in addition to the first. These two and the third candle were lighted by one of the children on the next Saturday evening, and finally, for the fourth week of Advent the last candle was made to burn with the other three. The advent wreath was a constant reminder to the children to live the Holy Season in a spirit of penance and expectation for the Christ Child.

The true pace of the holiday season was set, however, by the celebration of the feast of Saint Nicholas, December sixth. Dressed in episcopal robes, complete with mitre and staff, and accompanied by his servant, Knecht Ruprecht, the good saint visited the Hummel home as he visited the homes of most of the other children of Massing. From a great red book he read aloud the misdeeds of each little "bumble." Knecht Ruprecht who wore a fur cap and long fur cloak, had a switch but also carried a bag of gifts. One by one the children were called upon to pray and to give an account of their conduct during the past year. Berta was now old enough to enjoy this in her own way. Her ready wit and dry humor were at command. She feared neither the threatening rod nor the questions of the gruff visitor.

"Warst du auch gut?" "Have you been good?"

"Das Hummele ist immer gut." "The bumble is always good," commented her mother.

"Wenn ich schlaf." "When I'm asleep," came unsolicited from the fearless Berta.

Excitement and eagerness continued to grow as each day that was struck from the calendar brought Berta and her sisters and brothers nearer to Christmas. Everywhere, Markt Massing was taking on its holiday aspect. Christmas bazaars with their many booths and counters were set up. Here and there piles of fir trees stood ready for purchase, for even the poorest had their Christmas tree, the Tannenbaum, to be decorated with tinsel and artificial snow, with dainty wax figurines and tree ornaments, with gilded fruits and nuts purchased in the marketplace.

But of far greater importance was the erection of the crib. This year, Herr Hummel, just returned from army service, spent many grateful hours erecting and decorating the Bethlehem of the Hummel household.

By Christmas Eve the excitement had reached its height. After an early supper the children were sent upstairs while Frau Hummel and Lisi finished important tasks in the living room. At the appointed time the ringing of the Christmas bell brought the children in a rush down the stairs to the first floor. There under the towering tree were all the gifts they had requested. The Holy Child Jesus, the Kristkind, to Whom they had written all their wishes had left just the right thing for each of the six Hummel children. There was much laughing and screaming and general rejoicing until Lisi hustled them off to bed. The elders attended midnight Mass but the children rose early enough to take part in the Christmas procession before the five o'clock Mass. Later that day Berta with one of her sisters distributed gifts to the poor.

To Berta, the memories of Christmas with the crib and the tree were an inspiration which she did not allow to lie dormant. In this especially she succeeded in reviving the memory and depicting the real significance of the customs associated with this religious festival. Her Christmas cards and figurines have been instrumental in leading the way back to Bethlehem— to the Christ Child, His Mother Mary, and Saint Joseph.

But the snatches of holiday joy were not the only respite to break the routine in the everyday life of Berta Hummel. Spring brought Lent with its culmination in Holy Week and Easter. The celebrations began on Palm Sunday when the family attended the High Mass at which was blessed the palm branches carried to the church by Ady. Berta was up early on Palm Sunday because the local saying had it that whoever was last out of bed that morning should be dubbed the "Palm Esel." Thus the week began. During the days before Holy Thursday Berta was busy putting all her artistic abilities to use for the coming celebrations. She decorated baskets and boxes with colored paper, ribbons and laces. Later in the week she ornamented Easter eggs with her own designs and original decorations. A village tradition bears a special blessing for eggs produced on Holy Thursday and Good Friday. The former are decorated for Easter; the latter are used at the Good Friday meal. The Easter egg for her father bore an image of the Paschal Lamb holding aloft its victorious banner; that for her mother had a cross garlanded with lilies. On the eggs for her brothers and sisters she painted rabbits and chicks, while that for little Franzl had an ABC design. There were gifts also for "Hochwürden," her pastor, and for Sister Theresilla.

Meanwhile Berta attended all the religious ceremonies held at Saint Stephen's during Holy Week. With her brothers and sisters she visited the various wayside Calvaries and the parish Repository, where according to the custom, each child placed a floral offering before the Savior's tomb. Good Friday found the Hummel home reverent and quiet as was the entire town of Massing for all were bent on commemorating the sacred events. On Holy Saturday, the Hummels again brought to the church the palm branches that had been blessed the preceding Sunday. There the stems were charred in the sacred fire that was struck from flint and steel in the courtyard of the church that morning. After the service a flame from this fire was carried home together with the palms, which were then fashioned into small crosses. In the evening there was the solemn Resurrection service.

On Easter morning all were up before sunrise and ready for church. Berta was permitted to carry the Easter basket—which she herself had designed—containing portions of the food to be eaten at breakfast that morning: the Easter lamb baked by Lisi in a special mold, colored eggs, salt, and cakes. At the church these were blessed in solemn ceremony. This delightful little procession Berta portrayed in one of her most popular pictures—a chubby little girl in red pinafore and beribboned pigtails, clutching in one hand a bunch of field flowers, while gazing intently at the huge basket hung on her right arm. Lovingly and proudly she carries her precious burden, the Lamb with its victorious banner, the colored Easter eggs, and fruit.

27

The return home on Easter morning also had its thrills. A pious legend tells that on Easter morn the sun leaps three times at sunrise to greet its Risen Lord. With childish credulity, Berta was sure she had seen the phenomenon. Having returned home, while Frau Hummel and Lisi busied themselves preparing the Easter meal, Berta and her brothers and sisters began exploring for Easter nests. During the past three weeks there had been frequent "finds" in garden, barnyard, attic, and cellar, but on Easter morning the nest contained not only colored and chocolate eggs, but a gift as well.

Later that day the Hummels had a family reunion on the ancestral farm. There they took part in the farm procession which was always an event for the farmers of that region. Led by one of their number carrying a large cross, all the household and farmhands went singing and praying in procession about the cornfield. Small crosses of blessed palm were scattered throughout the route and finally the large cross was planted in the middle of the field. At each of the four corners the procession halted to strew egg shells left from Easter breakfast. All this was done very solemnly and prayerfully in the nature of a religious service, symbolic of fertility. The feastday supper followed, and then the visitors went home, each having been the recipient of a red Easter egg from grandfather, the customary gift to every visitor on this holiday.

Although Berta thoroughly enjoyed these religious celebrations, child that she was, she always looked forward with keen enthusiasm to the folk festivals with their boisterous abandon and their bustling activity. Her favorite at this period was the "Waldfest" or forest carnival carried on in Massing's own style. An improvised "Bierkeller" was set up in a shady wood near the church. Here tables and benches were arranged, and the special features and big attractions put in operation. The ten-pin balls rolled constantly and there was much shouting and general hilarity. A merry-go-round kept turning to the tune of an old musicbox melody and the children continued to ride as long as their pennies lasted. The rope-walkers and side shows held all spellbound. But the greatest thrill of the day was the ride on the Rott. The river presented a lively spectacle. A special steamer had been built for the occasion, and the townsfolk could ride along the banks of the picturesque stream. The water-bicycles were the center of special interest. They were propelled in such a manner that one could keep himself above water. The experience was quite exciting and had particular attraction for Berta who liked daring feats. Indeed, the carnival was a high-spot in Berta's life.

These were big events in the life of the child of Massing and she drew from them all the wealth of fun and experience that they offered. She was an active little girl who enjoyed nature and partook heartily in the amusements of her town and countryside. Berta was an adept on ice-skates, and with her companions revelled in the winter sports of Massing: ice-hockey on the Rott, sledding, skiing, skating,—but dreamy artist that she could be, she was just as contented to spend happy hours of a winter evening at the fireside, listening to Grimm's Fairy tales or the stories of the "Schwarzwald."

Chapter Four

SIMBACH

BERTA was twelve years old when she realized her dearest wish, admission to Simbach, the Institute of the "Englischen Fräulein," famous throughout Germany for its culture and learning. Simbach on the Inn River was a secondary school for girls located near the town of Braunau in the southeast corner of Germany. It was not far distant from Massing.

The Englischen Fräulein were teaching Sisters who conducted schools throughout Germany. They were founded by Mary Ward, a young English woman, who during the persecutions of the Catholics in the sixteenth century, had founded a congregation of teaching religious at St. Omer in France. The congregation met with much opposition, since its rule, based mainly on that of the Jesuits, allowed an active way of life entirely new at that time. Nevertheless, the religious conquered the obstacles raised against them and in the next one hundred and fifty years established schools throughout England, Germany, Ireland, Flanders, and

Italy. In 1877 they were given full ecclesiastical approbation. They devoted themselves mainly to the education of girls in boarding schools and academies, but also conducted primary and secondary schools, teacher training institutes, trade and domestic schools, and orphanages.

One of the original foundations of the Englischen Fräulein was at Burghausen, Germany. In 1909 this institute sent Sisters to Marienhöhe at Simbach on the Inn to begin a foundation there. The site was ideal. The convent building was erected in the midst of a beautiful park with shady lanes and groves, athletic fields, spacious orchards, and stretches of country for outdoor sports and recreation. A great iron bridge linked the institute with the city of Braunau on the Austrian border.

In the annals of Simbach two dates of special interest are still preserved: May 5, 1921 and July 4, 1927, the enrollment and withdrawal dates of Berta Hummel. Simbach had always been the young girl's ambition. The school had particular attraction for Berta because Viki and Käthi were attending there and their letters home were full of interest and enthusiasm. Then, too, Ady was at Marienhöhe attending the boys' school which was also conducted by the Englischen Fräulein.

Upon her entrance, Berta was enrolled in the lyceum or secondary course of studies. Because she was somewhat older than the average student she was permitted to enter the second year. With the help of private coaching and by serious application she was soon able to make the grades. Here again as at Massing, Berta was most interested and most proficient in art. Now as before, she could best express herself graphically. The school had a well-established art department and she was given every opportunity it offered to develop her talent. Reserved and unostentatious about her

31

work, she was accepted equally by both schoolmates and teachers. Just as she became one of the group in appearance, by donning the black school uniform with velvet collar, white blouse, and green belt, so she quickly identified herself with the interests and projects of the school.

Life at Simbach closely resembled the organizational character of most boarding schools. The day was well regulated with carefully scheduled activities in prayer, study, and recreation. At five-thirty each morning the bell called all the students for rising. On Wednesdays, designated "Ausschlafstag," the girls could sleep as long as they wished. At six o'clock all were in line for a study period before Holy Mass. The students were encouraged to make the best use of this favorable time for study which was usually spent out of doors if the weather permitted. Although not physically strong, Berta faithfully observed this early morning routine. Breakfast was followed by a succession of classes one hour in length, with a fifteen-minute intermission at ten o'clock. After the noon meal the students enjoyed a free period until two o'clock, when the regular routine continued as in the morning.

There were, of course, both planned and unforseen occasions that broke the regularity of these school days. Sunday afternoon walks, feastday picnics, weekly excursions. These were welcome diversions that Berta enjoyed with the rest of the students. It always meant seeing something new, coming closer to nature with all the beauties and secrets that it held. Returning from a trip to the neighboring wood or the Alps, Berta could easily be identified by her armful of trophies in flowers, foliage, and other interesting finds. Usually these found their way to a favorite grotto or shrine.

It was the custom at Marienhöhe that when students reached the fourth year they be permitted to become

Children of Mary. The feast of the Immaculate Conception, December eighth, was the day of reception. The religious service was held in the morning. In the afternoon there was usually a play performed by the students in the recreation hall. Berta always had a hand in these affairs. When not actually taking part in the play, she was indispensable for decorating, staging, costuming. What was missing in scenery or properties, she supplied; she never lacked a substitute. Trees or bushes, capitals of columns, wings for angels, all seemed to spring from nowhere. There was no delay, no fuss or confusion; she worked like a veteran stagehand.

When the interior of the school proved inadequate for the scope of her constructive art, she set to work outside. An attractive feature of the campus at Simbach was an Alpine rock garden with miniature mountain scenery. For some time a beautifully illuminated giant mushroom crowned the peak, serving as a shelter and cozy nook. Berta had designed this landscape decoration. Later she modeled in clay a beautiful deer, reposing lifelike on the peak.

The roguish Berta of Volkschule days who loved to mimic and caricature with pencil and paper was also in evidence at Simbach. The tendency certainly had not diminished; if anything, it had become almost an obsession. She would sketch a rapid profile and then pass it around for identification; or she would manage to catch one or the other Sister or Mistress in an unusual situation and immediately reproduce it on paper. At one time she sketched her physical education teacher, for whom she had a genuine respect and affection, wearing a big garden hat and in the act of throwing the ball across the Turnhalle floor.

One of the keepsakes treasured at Simbach is a series of sketches done by Berta in connection with her work in the literature class. Anyone who has read and enjoyed Weber's DREIZEHN LINDEN will appreciate her ingenious illustrations of that classic. DREIZEHN LINDEN is a collection of poems having their historic background in the sagas of the Old Germanic gods. The fables and stories offered rich material for illustration and Berta's skill and interpretation afforded her an opportunity of revealing much which would otherwise have remained obscured.

Berta's art work was now beginning to show a firmness of stroke and a deepening of understanding that reflected the physical and mental development concomitant with adolescence. Pencil and brush were the media that objectified the creations of her active imagination. Her pictures now began to exhibit a tender spiritual expression that gave promise of an innate wealth of soul and a richness and depth of spiritual values. There could be no doubt about Berta's future career; her talent and her keenest interests were in the field of visual beauty.

Chapter Five

SOJOURN AT MUNICH

WHEN Berta Hummel graduated from Simbach on the feast of Our Lady's Annunciation, March 25, 1926, she was ready for matriculation at Munich. For years Herr Hummel had been hoping that some day he could give his daughter the opportunity of study at one of the great art schools. Munich met the stipulations of his desire to do the best for Berta, and even during her course at Simbach he planned for her eventual entrance into the Art Academy of that city. He himself, therefore, accompanied her on the fifty-mile journey from Massing and saw her safely established in her new environment.

During the years of Berta Hummel's study there, Munich ranked with the best cities of Europe in the opportunities it offered to the earnest art student. It was not only the home of some of the finest teachers and most successful artists, but it continually gave inspiration in the beauty of its public buildings, its churches, galleries, monuments, gardens, and palaces.

The interiors of many of these buildings contained unrivalled paintings, frescoes, statues, and murals. The wealth of the city's art treasure, both in buildings and in decorative masterpieces, was the accumulation of centuries.

Originally a settlement of monks, "Mönche," from whence its name, "München" was first mentioned early in the twelfth century. Like most European cities, it passed through a series of wars, conflagrations, and changes of rulers, each leaving some historic impression that was to distinguish its character from that of every other German city. With the establishment of the Wittelbacher rulers in the nineteenth century, Munich underwent a period of growth and beautification. Under the patronage of these sovereigns New Munich came into being to add vitality and grace to the ancient splendor of the Old. Magnificent buildings of every style of architecture, handsome boulevards and wide streets, carefully laid gardens and richly ornamented squares, colossal statues and artistic columns made the city, not only one of the most beautiful, but likewise one of the most interesting of Europe. The influence and activity of the Wittelbacher rulers drew to Munich artists and artisans of every station: painters, sculptors, architects; connoisseurs, musicians, and scholars—all destined to add their contribution in the process of transforming the prosaic medieval town into a modern city of vast proportions and diversity of interest.

The presence of so much culture and refinement did not, however, make Munich a solemn city. Its citizens were noted for their carefreeness and gaity. During the carnival season in January and February the spirit of the people became one of unrestrained hilarity. The "Oktoberfest" likewise made one huge playground of the city. In general the population had always been composed of immigrants rather than of native born:

happy, vivacious, optimistic, inclining especially toward material comfort, without however laying claim to excessive luxury and elegance, but by no means content with scanty fare. Upright and sincere, conservative and reluctant for innovation, the citizens of Munich paid little attention to social distinction. The city's spirit of cordial hospitality made the stranger soon feel at home and readily prolong his stay there.

This was the city to which Berta Hummel came in the fall of 1927 to begin her four years of art study in preparation for her future career. She was eighteen years old, ambitious, talented, hopeful, eager to be a success. She was not going to be satisfied with mere instruction; she would visit every haunt and corner of this resourceful city to glean for herself whatever it had to offer for her growth and development.

At first Berta occupied a small room in the vicinity of the convent of Saint Ann. Life there proved to be more distracting than she cared to have it, so after a short time she sought a more quiet and secluded study. She took up residence at Holy Family, a convent of Sisters located in the Blumenstrasse near the beautiful church of Our Lady, the Frauenkirche. Here she lived as "Heimchen," as the boarders were called. Her daily walk to the Art Academy led her along the Marienstrasse past the Frauenkirche, one of the ancient buildings of Munich. This Gothic church dates back to the fifteenth century. Its twin towers culminate in huge domes which give its exterior a somewhat clumsy appearance. Its interior, however, is a thing of beauty; exquisite art windows, an expansive nave with twenty pillars, majestic statues—these are only a portion of the beauty that rewards the visitor or worshipper. Berta made frequent visits to this church out of a spirit of devotion more than for artistic reasons, because she realized that, sheltered as she had been by reason of her small-town background and convent education, she needed the special guidance and protection of Mary, most pure Virgin, to withstand the temptations of the gay and worldly city. She was lively, affectionate, and fun-loving by natural temperament, but she was also reserved, prudent, and thoughtful. She was accommodating and sociable and by reason of her cleverness was a general favorite in the get-togethers for the girls at Holy Family. Although she was never strong physically, she worked with steady, constant application, her strength seeming to come more from enthusiasm than from physical energy.

Even the students at this quiet boarding convent could not be unaware and entirely uninfluenced by the merrymaking of Mardi Gras. Usually they planned some little celebration of their own, since many of them, like Berta, had grown up with the South Bavarian tradition of Mardi Gras festivities as part of their childhood lore. Their demonstrations, however, were greatly restrained because of their residence at the convent and the rules that the institute imposed on the boarders. One year Berta held her friends and superiors in suspense for several weeks with enigmatic explanations of the special feature she was preparing for Mardi Gras.

One day she approached the Mother Superior with apparent hesitancy and asked the latter to grant her a special favor.

"Yes, Fräulein Hummel, if such is within my power and not contrary to the rules of the school, I shall certainly do what I can for you."

Berta feigned to divulge a great secret. "We are going to have special visitors for Mardi Gras, Mother. May we make special preparations?"

"Who might these visitors be, and what special preparations would their coming mean?"

"I cannot tell you now, Mother; it is a secret. They are important and lovely people, precious friends,

Sister Innocentia's Infant of Krumbad.

Hummel Madonnas.

XV

whose coming would make me and all the students very happy. Please Mother, do trust me and give me permission to have them."

"Unless I know who these visitors are, Fräulein Berta, I cannot give you permission. I would not know what sort of preparation their entertaining would require."

"Leave it to me, Mother, I know what will be needed, and I promise there will be no extra burden on the house."

"You are not planning to have any gentlemen here, Berta? You know Mardi Gras has always been a family feast. The Fräulein love to masquerade. There is so much fun in trying to identify the individual characters and to select the best costumes for prizes."

"I know that too, Mother, but just for this one time, please."

"There will be no secrets, dear child. I am always willing to help where the happiness of our girls is concerned. But I have the responsibility of knowing what is going on in the school. Your parents expect that, Fräulein, so that is final."

With that the good nun turned to go but Berta restrained her.

"Please Mother, I will tell just you, but you cannot refuse now. I have already invited the guests."

Mother looked anxious but the twinkle in Berta's eyes made her promise. "For this one time only, but who are these special visitors?"

Berta drew a deep breath; then bending closer she whispered: "All my professors from the Art Academy: Professor Dasio, Professor Wirnhier, Professor Klein and, of course, Madame Professor Brauneis." Seeing the consternation in Mother Superior's face, she added, "I will take care of everything, Mother. Just leave it to me."

Dubiously the kind Sister shook her head and then went about her duties. "Fräulein Hummel is so winsome. One cannot refuse her anything. But this is an innovation—the Fräulein will lose their heads."

Berta had scored another point and she was feverishly restless getting ready for the great occasion. Mardi Gras was fast approaching and the suspense grew from hour to hour. Everyone knew that something unusual was to happen, for the zealous Mistress had reiterated again and again at the etiquette class the necessity of decorum, poise, and good manners. The reputation of the institute must be upheld.

At last the eventful evening arrived. The reassuring smile on Berta's face did not quite remove the anxiety and perturbation of the Superior. Anxiously she awaited the clang of the bell which would announce the guests. Fräulein Hummel would receive them—there was no need to worry on that score. Everybody but Mother was in a joyous mood. The students suspected that important guests were expected, but no one knew who they might be.

Presently the ominous bell sounded and a few moments later Berta, radiant and happy, announced that the visitors were awaiting the girls and the Mistress in the parlor. All were due for a surprise, but for the good Mistress relief was uppermost. Arranged in colorful parade in the parlor were miniature statues representing Berta's professors skillfully modeled in plastics and dressed quite properly each in his own peculiar costume. There was much merriment that evening after the group had sufficiently recovered from their surprise and admiration.

As is customary in boarding schools the girls were responsible for the condition of their respective rooms. The bed must be without a wrinkle, the floors and furniture innocent of a particle of dust, the wardrobe without unnecessary accumulation. In the case of

40

Berta those rules and regulations frequently occasioned amusing situations. The Mistress would often throw up her hands in despair when she entered Berta's room. An orderly disorder held sway. There was no more appropriate place to spread out her drawings than the bed, the windowsills, the very places which the meticulous Sister tabooed as being against all rules and regulations. The incongruous earmark of so many artists failed to impress and conciliate the tidy and exact little nun. But she loved Fräulein Hummel almost to a fault, in spite of all her worries. With real and unfeigned sympathy she would waive her own ideals and carefully find a place for each stray sketch, unruly brush, and messy pan, often also, to the chagrin of the girl, who knew just where she had left that sketch to dry. Staunchly the admirers of Berta Hummel at Holy Family maintained that even the valleys and hills of her rumpled bed cover had a certain amount of the artistic in their irregularity.

There was another of those vexing boarding school rules that Berta considered to be quite a hardship. The nuns were very insistent on silence in the corridors. Noisy, saucy heels savored of bustle and confusion. Berta really did want to please everyone, but the "Hummele" in her made it so natural for her to bumble and hurry without much thought of how her walk sounded! The halls were so susceptible to sound. Why didn't the Sisters install noiseless flooring? They, of course, knew how to walk slowly and sedately.

"Fräulein Hummel, please step quietly."

"Berta, do walk slowly."

"Fräulein Hummel, will you ever learn to walk sedately?"

But really, they would not have had her otherwise.

Meanwhile, Berta was becoming more and more engrossed in her work at the Art Academy. On April

25, 1927, she passed a brilliant examination in the
Academy of Plastic Arts, and although one of the
youngest, she rated second in the finals. Her name was
familar in every department. She studied portrait
painting under Professor Dasio and Professor Wirnhier; color and composition under Professor Klein;
water color under Madame Else Brauneis. Professor
Dasio had great esteem for Berta's work and chal-
lenged some of his less ambitious students to imitate
her skill and drive. He later wrote to Frau Hummel:
"Your daughter Berta was one of the dearest, most
talented and later most successful of my many students."

In a like way, Madame Else Brauneis recognized
Berta's talent and formed an intimate friendship with
her. In the excursions about Munich and to the neighboring points of interest, Madame Brauneis observed
Berta closely and shared ideas and appreciations with
her. Later she wrote concerning her:

"With most of my students, when I recognized them
as sincere and earnest, I entertained a social friendship. Berta was very close to me, but because of her
intensive program, we had little time to talk about anything other than that pertained to her work. Highly
intelligent and gifted with extraordinary talent, the
young girl felt obligated to work more zealously and
more intensively than the rest. She showed great joy
and enthusiasm for all things beautiful.

"On several occasions she accompanied us when the
class in aquarelles visited Lindau and Salzburg. She
sketched and worked continuously during such tours,
and I regret that so little time was left for intimate
conversation, since correcting and advising took up all
our allotted time.

"On our way to and from the place of studies we
were again occupied in observing nature, so personal
references were at a minimum. Thus I came to know

little about my favorite student beyond our mutual interests.

"After she had successfully and brilliantly passed her examinations as teacher of art, I, with the rest of the faculty, cherished the hope of her returning to the Academy.

"But one day she visited my home to inform me that other plans were preventing her returning to Munich. Thus ended for a time all personal contact; even our correspondence was of necessity limited."

During the time of her stay at Holy Family, Berta Hummel formed a friendship that was to have a very marked influence on the subsequent character of her life. Two Franciscan Sisters from the Convent at Siessen came to Munich to work for their degree at the Art Academy. Berta was asked to assist them in adjusting themselves to their new environment: acquaint them with helpful people, introduce them to the circle of artists, plan their tours about Munich. As she became more intimate with Sister Laura and Sister Kostka, the young girl began to study carefully the lives and characters of these two friends. They were devoted, exemplary Religious; nevertheless, they were artists— ambitious, eager, gifted. She saw that their religious profession in no way hindered the exercise of their talent; on the contrary, it seemed to make them freer, removing all purely material responsibilities, leaving them full scope to prepare for a career that was definite and that would develop their natural gifts.

Berta, too, was ambitious. She dreamed of traveling to Italy, to Spain, to France, to see with her own eyes the works of the great masters. She wanted to come under the influence of the leading teachers of the day, to be guided by their instruction, fired by their inspiration. Berta wanted to be a success, and she wanted to see the day when her work would reach such a point of acceptance that it would be sought for outside of

Massing and Munich, even outside of Germany. Her prospects were not discouraging. Even now at her graduation, March 15, 1931, her six professors sought her with as much ardor as ever handsome knight wooed fair lady, each hopeful that she would continue study under his direction. Graduated first in her class, her future was promising. With good reason, everyone expected much of her. Although she surprised them, she did not disappoint them.

Chapter Six

THE DIVINE CALL

BERTA lingered long before the Virgin's altar in the Frauenkirche on the Marienstrasse. Morning after morning on her way to the Art Academy she had paused for a brief visit with the Eucharistic Lord and His Blessed Mother. Today she had come to thank them for the success that had rewarded her work of the past four years. She knew and acknowledged how much of the glory belonged to God and how insufficient were her own efforts. There were bright prospects before her. All her teachers assured her of the genuineness of her talent and the success she could anticipate were she to continue as she had worked and achieved during these past years in Munich.

Nevertheless, Berta's mind was not occupied solely with the satisfaction of success. She was trying to resolve a problem that had for some time been asserting itself, and she knew she must now come to a decision. The truth is, Berta Hummel was undergoing a struggle between her natural relish for the sweetness of the world's applause and the supernatural hunger

45

for values higher than the merely material. She felt
called to serve God in religious life. The thought of
final dedication to the service of God was continually
intruding into her brightest dreams of a brilliant future in the career she had planned.

The intimate companionship with Sister Laura and
Sister Kostka had revealed to her how beautifully these
two Religious had reconciled a similar double ambition. They were good Religious; but they were artists,
too, avidly seeking to better themselves in their profession. They were virtuous and faithful to a minute
rule of life that regulated their day very precisely;
but they were happy, tranquil, eager to enjoy all the
beauty that was theirs to have.

But she was Berta Hummel, who had tasted at least
a little of the world's applause. She had seen her
creations admired by no mean critics. She was supremely happy in her art, and she had promise that a
rosy path to fame lay before her. Surely, she should
not mar the happiness of her graduation with thoughts
that suggested such sacrifice. Had she studied so hard
to bury herself and her talents in obscurity? And she
loved Munich—loved it intensely for all that it had
meant to her. No, surely God would not expect so
much of her now, since He had helped her thus far on
the road to success. She could serve Him faithfully
in the world; such she had tried to do as long as she
could recall.

Then she pictured herself in the pattern of life of
her two Franciscan artist-friends. As a Religious, she
could paint. True, she would not be able to rove at
will. She might be hampered in her ambitions; perhaps she would not be given the chance to see Italy, and
Spain, and France. But as a Religious, her cherished
ambitions would be, not frustrated, but encouraged.
The day would be regulated; she would not be able to

46

Sister Innocentia was happiest when with the children.

Sister Innocentia's Convent Chapel at Siessen.

Institut Kloster Siessen bei Saulgau (Württbg.) vom Flugzeug aus

Sister Innocentia's Convent at Siessen.

Sister Innocentia's Studio at the Convent at Siessen.

St. Conrad

(In Parish Church at Massing)

One of Berta's favorite saints, St. Therese of Lisieux.

paint just as she pleased, but the hours of quiet contemplation, of meditation on Him, the Source of all Beauty, would be a reservoir of strength and inspiration. She would be one of many—garbed and trained and directed as scores of the other "Schwestern," and seemingly unidentifiable from the rest. Yet, she could still create; she could still see and love God in her own way in every one of His creatures; in the bird, the bush, the bee, the tree, the flower; in the eyes of His little ones. Not always, perhaps, could she paint with pallet and brush, but at least she could delineate His image in the hearts of those entrusted to her care. It was hard to resist the attractions of a successful career; it was even more difficult to refuse the inner promptings of grace. Only one who has known the heart-rending struggle between doubt and fear can realize the agonizing indecision that is to be endured in the spiritual combat of a soul striving to sever the heartstrings from all that she once loved and cherished, because there is an irresistible something that will take no half-hearted sacrifice. The conflict can be appreciated only by those who have conquered in that struggle.

But for Berta the battle was as brief as it was intense; and for her, to decide was to do. She would serve God unstintingly as she believed He was asking her to serve Him. She made her tryst with her Sacramental Lord, and then experienced an untold peace, supreme calm, and joy. Her greatest pain now lay in the obligation she felt toward her loved ones. Reflecting on the sacrifices her parents had made for her interests, she longed to repay them. Her teachers, too, had spent themselves in developing her talents; they expected great things from her. Indeed, the call to religious life brought keen sacrifice.

Berta's parents were not too much surprised to learn of their daughter's decision, but neither were they unaware of all she was relinquishing in her choice.

Nevertheless, pious Christians that they were, they hesitated to resist the designs of an all-wise Providence. They felt keenly the separation from their daughter in whom they had placed such great hope, but they agreed to take no step in opposition to her decision.

"Berta is not strong enough for such a strenuous life," mused practical Herr Hummel. "Will she be able to live under the severe rule of a convent? She is so frail and delicate."

"God never asks more of us than we can do," humbly returned his wife. "God chooses the weak things of this world to confound the strong. What others have done, our Berta can also do. Are there no privations in other walks of life?"

"But she is so lively; she must sing, and run, and joke. She is a Hummele. To put her in a convent cell is like putting a little creature into a cage."

"Have you ever seen a real monk or nun unhappy, Adolf? Saint Francis was one of the happiest of God's creatures."

"But her talents, Victoria; her genius. Must she bury these? Are we sure she will be permitted to use her gifts and all the training she has had?"

"No, we are not sure. God may also ask that sacrifice of our child along with all that she holds dear. But does not a woman, for the sake of the man she loves, often give up her career, all her ambitions in order to devote herself to the service of her husband and family? I am sure no greater sacrifice is demanded from a girl when she is called by God to the religious life than is asked from the young woman who takes her responsibilities seriously when she marries."

The case being such, the good couple really saw no problem, because ultimately they willed to do God's

Will as faithfully as Berta wished to do It. Her decision was but the reflection of the training they had given her, a reaction to all the pious little customs and traditions of her childhood; truly an answer to their own prayers for the well-being of this their child.

But Berta's troubles did not end with the consent of her parents. There were other sources that were loathe to be robbed of promising talent; there were those who would judge her motives, who would imply false and unkind judgment because they did not understand. Berta had lived the cultural life of Munich with evident zest and pleasure. She had not been a recluse. Although she had not joined in the boisterous, heyday activities of some of the art students, she had lived a normal life, enjoying those recreations and pleasures that her sunny temperament demanded. Her unusual decision, therefore, estranged some; they wondered under what influence this action was fostered.

"That girl has been influenced by those who will profit by her popularity."

"She is ungrateful to her parents and to those who have been instrumental in her success."

Tongues wagged and Berta knew she was the target of criticism. She had meant to keep her secret and to retire unnoticed and in peace, but that was not possible.

Shortly before her entrance into the convent Berta, dressed in a new and attractive outfit, was met by one of her acquaintances.

"You have apparently given up the idea of going to the convent, Berta?"

"Not in the least. I am growing more eager every day."

"But your clothes—you have always loved nice things. And those you are wearing now—don't you think they are somewhat extravagant for one who contemplates giving up all?"

"I shall continue my way of living till I enter the convent. Never have I been conscious of offending God by my attire. Why should I fear doing so now?"

"Then Munich did not take the idea from your mind?"

"Munich has made me more determined than ever."

"Will you be allowed to continue the study of art in the cloister?"

"I do not know, but I am indifferent. I wish only to serve God and humanity, and I feel I can best accomplish His Holy Will as a Religious, so I am willing to give up all to fulfill my chosen vocation."

Berta's next step was her choice of convent. This was not an easy matter. She loved the Poor School Sisters who conducted the Volkschule in Massing. Then there were the Englischen Fräulein at Simbach. How happy she was when she recalled those favorite teachers and intimate chums of her girlhood at boarding school! There were the Sisters of the Holy Family in the Blumenstrasse. They had been very good to her when she lived there as "Heimchen." But more than all this, there was the intimate association with her two Franciscan companions from Siessen who had studied with her at the Art Academy. They had worked and prayed with her; they, in particular, had proved to her that it was possible to be a good Religious and to follow her cherished ambition. They were, furthermore, daughters of Saint Francis, whose ideals and character were so much like her own; who saw the Creator in all His creatures; whose spirit sang, though his body was racked with pain; who was the troubadour of the great King. A temperament such as hers was readily attracted to the Poor Man of Assisi. She therefore resolved to apply for admission to the convent of the Franciscan Sisters at Siessen in Württemberg. There was probably another factor which, according to Berta's mother, was one of the chief motives for selecting the convent at Siessen. It was the fact that among the Franciscans all Sisters were equal; there were no lay and choir Sisters. This was entirely in the spirit of Berta Hummel, who saw God in all His creatures, even the most humble. Some time after Berta's entrance Frau Hummel was accosted by one of the Sisters employed in the garden, and who was consequently not so well educated as those who were degreed teachers.

"Do you know, Frau Hummel," she said, "Your daughter, Sister Innocentia, loves us simple Sisters better than the rest?"

Having made her choice of convent at Siessen, Berta next sought admission. The history of this community dates back to the Middle Ages. Soon after the death of Saint Dominic in 1221, there arose in Württemberg, a province of southern Germany, eleven convents of nuns professing the rule of Saint Dominic. Among these was one at Saulgau. The estate was called Siessen which means pasture or meadowland. It was presented to six Dominican nuns by one of the counts of the Steinmar dynasty. In the fourteenth century the estate expanded and by 1452 the convent had attained definite renown.

Unfortunately little is known of the religious life of this first community, but by the sixteenth century a reform was imperative. When but four nuns were left in the convent in 1567, four Dominican nuns came from Pforzheim to augment and revive the moribund community. The convent began to flourish anew, but the seventeenth century brought additional vicissitudes. Four times the Sisters were forced to flee: in 1632, when the Swedes burnt the buildings to the ground; in 1674, when fire destroyed the restored buildings; in 1688, when the French forced their way into the country and the convent was evacuated; and finally in 1702, during the Spanish insurrection.

51

With peace restored the community pursued its life of prayer and charity under the direction of their Prioress Mary Dominica Baizin. This able woman erected numerous buildings and finally established the "Okonomie," a counterpart of the American Academy. The finances of Siessen were now on a sound basis and the convent grew and flourished until the secularization of religious houses in 1803. During this period when the property of the Church and of religious was seized and sold for the profit of the state, Siessen fell to the lot of the princes of Turin and Taxis.

Fifty-seven years later, in 1860, a community of Franciscan nuns came into control of the affairs at Siessen. This congregation had been founded just seven years previous at Oggelheuren. At the time when they took over Siessen, one Dominican nun was living in the convent. A new life began; the Franciscan congregation flourished in spite of storms and strife.

At the outbreak of World War II the community numbered eight hundred religious in charge of sixty-five educational institutions. From 1860 to 1935 Siessen had its own Teachers' Seminary; from 1924 to 1935 there were special classes for the training of housekeepers. Beginning in 1920 the Sisters devoted themselves to the care of the sick. The renown of Siessen embroidery is worldwide, and the convent has gained additional prestige in the work and reputation of Sister Innocentia.

It was at Siessen, then, that Berta Hummel sought admission. She had visited the Motherhouse with Sister Laura and Sister Kostka a few weeks before, so she was not now a total stranger. The Reverend Mother received her kindly and asked a few questions regarding her qualifications. Berta reassured her that she was ready to do anything the rule required. Her art? She loved it, but she wanted to love God above everything and serve Him as He willed. Her health? She was not strong, but she had never been ill or off duty. She always loved to work. Yes, she liked to pray and she believed she could conform to the convent's rule of life. She admitted that her parents were sad, but resigned. No, they did not need her support.

Having been formally accepted as a candidate, Berta chose April 22, 1931, five weeks after her graduation, as her entrance day. The parting from home and loved ones was touching, but it was made beautiful in the brave Christian resignation of the parents and the happy anticipation of the young girl.

Berta carried into the convent her sunny disposition and her love of fun. Her superiors liked her candor, her humble obedience, her cheerfulness. The Bumble Bee had become, indeed, the humble bee of Saint Francis. It must not be presumed, however, that she slipped automatically into this new environment. She was accustomed to freedom and spontaneity as conditions of her happiness, and she had to make many adjustments in her new life. In the precincts of the convent, one's time belonged to God. There was much to be done and every duty was regulated by obedience. One worked and prayed, recreated and kept silence at the sound of the bell. Throughout the day there were definite times and places for silence—not, of course, a rigid silence that forbade necessary intercourse, but only such as would restrain from useless gossip that led to loss of time and recollection.

Even during the days of her novitiate Berta's talent was encouraged by her religious superiors. She continued her creative work at the same time that she prepared herself to instruct the children. Through the use of her greeting cards and holiday designs the convent continued to spread her work and name. She was supremely happy when, in company with her two Sister friends of Munich days, she was permitted to attend the art exhibit held at Beuron, where some of her own work was on display. The Beuron School of Art under the administration of the Benedictine Fathers has a world-wide reputation and attracts many students and scholars to its lovely studios.

Two years of religious life passed quickly and Berta with thirty companions was ready to be clothed in the habit of Saint Francis. The reception took place on the feast of the Immaculate Heart of Mary, August 22, 1933. The centuries-old convent church was packed with worshippers—relatives and friends who had come for the impressive ceremony. The Hummels were there, seven strong: Herr Hummel and his wife, their three daughters and two sons. It was a great day for them, one of supreme sacrifice but poignant happiness. The service began with the procession of the candidates up the long aisle to their places before the altar. At the Offertory the thirty postulants advanced slowly and reverently into the sanctuary to ask for the habit of the Sisters of the Third Order of Saint Francis. As each knelt in turn before him, the Bishop significantly cut off a lock of hair, symbolic of the renouncement of earthly vanity, and placing a crucifix in her hand, bestowed on her a new name.

Sister Maria Innocentia! The name was appropriate, significant. Innocentia Hummel! She had loved the innocence of childhood, she who herself showed such childlike simplicity was henceforth to be known to her Sisters only as Sister Maria Innocentia. Her name and early reputation would continue; the world would remember her as Berta Hummel, but now she truly had another name for she was espoused to One she loved and would serve forever, the King of heaven and earth.

Some of the Famous Hummel Cards.

XVI

Ample Chasubles designed by Berta.

The exhibit of her work that had been held at Beuron was now, on the day of her reception, on display at the Motherhouse. There were creations in charcoal, pastel, water color, and oil. In another hall was a display of handwork that she had designed. The exhibit was a great comfort to the young nun's parents, who were now convinced beyond doubt that Berta must be happy and contented in her vocation in order to accomplish so much work in so brief a space of time.

It was during the tranquil days of her novitiate that Sister Innocentia gave special attention to religious subjects in her art work. Although no longer under expert guidance, left solely to her own initiative, she showed great advance in creativeness and skill. Madame Else Brauneis, her instructor in water color at Munich, relates that although they retained a sincere friendship after Berta's departure for Siessen and also corresponded, she knew of the nun's work only in the greeting and postal cards which she saw in the stores. Only at the Memorial Exhibit held at Massing, August 1947, was her teacher made aware of the magnificent work she had done in other fields. Her large Madonnas, her church murals, banners, vestments, altar cards, all were her own creations fostered and developed without any other instruction. Madame Brauneis expressed her own wonder at what Sister Innocentia's development would have been, could she have studied just one year in Italy! During this year of probation while her health was poor, her strong will kept her at work.

A second step in her religious consecration took place on August 30, 1934. On this day Sister Innocentia pronounced her first vows. The ceremony of Profession was even more impressive than that of the clothing with the holy habit. At the appointed time the novices again entered the sanctuary and prostrated before the altar. A large cloth, significant of the death pall, was placed over their prostrate forms, while the clergy recited the Litany of the Saints. This spiritual dying was symbolic of the renouncement that the Religious had made of all earthly desires and ambitions. When the Litany ended, the Sisters rose, and with lighted candle in hand, knelt before the Bishop individually and solemnly bound themselves by vow to serve God in holy religion.

Sister Innocentia went back to her work and continued to form Christ in her own heart and life, while she imaged His creatures in her art creations. During those days her first children pictures were edited. Then followed Madonnas, a whole series of them; and finally, humorous subjects of every description. The children pictures, however, had established the Hummel fame. Perhaps nothing did more to spread the work of Sister Innocentia than the *Hummelbuch* published by her friend, Margareta Seeman, who moreover, enhanced the delightful work by her apt and witty interpretations in verse of some of the most humorous of the pictures.

The following story related by one of the intimates of Sister Innocentia will reveal the popularity of the *Hummelbuch* as well as give us an insight into the sweet modesty and retirement of the artist. On one occasion Sister Innocentia was enroute for Munich. Rosary in hand she sat engrossed in her meditations, when a middle-aged lady took a seat in the train directly opposite Sister. In her hand she held a copy of the recently published *Hummelbuch*. From time to time she would emit a shout of delight or an amused chuckle as she turned page after page of the attractive volume. Again and again she would exclaim: "Splendid"! "Unique"! "What originality!" Sister Innocentia smiled in modest amusement. Presently the lady rose, looked for a moment at the nun opposite her and then ventured: "Why Sister, you are wearing the same garb as does Sister Innocentia. Are you perhaps from the same Community?" "Yes," was the modest rejoinder, "I am from the same Community."

Thus the reputation of the young artist was being rapidly established, but Sister Innocentia strove only for the Master's glory and longed to be hidden and retired. Hardly a day passed when a visitor would not express the desire to see and converse with her. Naturally a limit had to be made and most of the requests had to be politely refused. On one occasion Sister Innocentia happened to be in the hall where her work was being exhibited and also offered for sale. A young man approached her and made known his grievance. "For a long time now it has been my earnest wish to see Sister Innocentia. Her art has captivated me. I have come a great distance and my disappointment at not being able to see her is not small." With a solicitude truly maternal Sister Innocentia comforted the young man, explaining that he must realize the impossibility of having Sister Innocentia interrupted every hour of the day. A nun has her duties, spiritual and temporal, and one cannot expect that she neglect anyone of them. Her encouraging conversation and her tender regard for his disappointment enabled her to cheer the young man and he went away comforted to examine and enjoy others of the pictures. After Sister Innocentia had left the hall, another Sister approached the man and said: "I see that you have been favored by a confidential chat with Sister Innocentia." Now only did he realize who his kindly comforter had been.

On another occasion a young teacher from the neighboring village of Mengen came to Siessen requesting an interview with Sister Innocentia. Himself artistically inclined, he stood on the threshold of her studio pleading for this favor. He had just been drafted into service and was wearing the uniform. Reluctantly Sister

Laura informed the disappointed young man that it was not possible to see the artist. She had secluded herself within her studio and had given orders not to be disturbed in the important work which she was planning. This was her usual plea of avoiding publicity. And in truth, all God's work is important. At this moment Sister Innocentia came fluttering up the corridor. Hearing the whispered conversation and seeing the soldier she drew near. "Ah, a uniform! How lovely! May I examine it? How does the buckle close? On which side is the gun-strap?" Beaming with inexpressible joy, the youthful tiro and teacher answered her questions with the docility of the humblest scholar. Several days later he received from Sister Innocentia the charming sketch showing two uniformed youngsters and the text: "Lieb Vaterland, magst ruhig sein." "Dear Fatherland, thou canst rest."

One of her vacation tours into Switzerland brought Sister Innocentia into Fribourg. Here she visited a girls' school conducted by the Sisters of Siessen. On her visit to the classrooms she came into the art room where classes were in progress. The class was highly enthusiastic for the work of Sister Hummel and spoke ardently of her charming cards and sketches. "If only once we could see Sister, show her our work and let her criticize it!" With a benign smile Sister Innocentia went from one to the other, praising and encouraging here, criticizing and helping there, giving practical and helpful hints in her modest, selfless fashion. After she had left, their teacher told the class who their kind visitor had been. Their joy knew no bounds and the visit will never be forgotten, yet there was not wanting a certain reproachful chagrin, because they had failed to surmise the charming personality of Sister Hummel.

Her modesty and love for solitude made her acutely conscious of every danger in the form of an unwelcome visitor. There were two doors to her studio. On hearing the Guest-Sister approach with a visitor, she noiselessly fluttered out of her studio and disappeared. But when charity or reverence demanded, she was sociable, as she was also whenever she realized that curiosity was not the motive of the visit. On one occasion a Sister was leading her ninety-year old mother through the house. The aged woman was an enthusiast of the Hummel art and expressed her desire for an autograph of the artist. Sister Innocentia rose at once, led her venerable guest to the showcase where her cards were on display and then with gracious deference said: "Which of the cards do you like best?" Without hesitation the old lady reached for the card bearing the text: *Gebet vor der Schlacht,* "The Prayer before the Battle." A little five-year old is about to mount his wooden horse. In realization of the gravity of the act, he first folds his hands devoutly, and with bowed head lisps a fervent prayer. The reverent attitude of the little fellow makes a deep impression on the beholder. Smilingly Sister Innocentia took the card, wrote a special greeting, and with a gracious smile gave it to her visitor.

This same little hero sketch was responsible for saving the vocation of a young deacon. It was his last step before ordination. Humbly he related how the struggles and temptations were well-nigh overwhelming and how he was already forming the resolution to give up a state of life which he felt was, at least in his case, beyond human possibility. But help came in a most unexpected way. By chance the little Hummel card depicting the praying child, came into his hands. The prayerful simplicity and earnest fervor of the little horseman, so serious before an important undertaking, brought the student to the realization that for him, the most necessary thing was prayer, fervent, constant prayer for help and guidance. With all the fervor of his soul he began to pray as he had never prayed before. God heard his humble plea; peace and light filled his soul. Today he is a fervent minister of God.

Sister Innocentia's modesty and retirement were balanced by a wholesome impetuosity and sense of humor. These characteristics were not a little responsible for some of her most charming sketches. On one glorious spring day there was a demand for general work in the Convent. "All who can get away from ordinary duties come into the field for weeding." So ran the invitation. This was always a welcome treat for the young novices and eagerly they pressed forward offering their services. As a matter of course Sister Innocentia stood ready for the task. The venerable mistress of novices looked kindly at the eager face before her, then shook her head thoughtfully: "No, child, you cannot go. The weather is too foggy and the work, too fatiguing. Go rather into your studio and offer your disappointment for the success of our work." It cannot be gainsaid that Sister Innocentia felt peeved at her inability to help with the other novices, but obediently she betook herself to her studio. But pull she must, even though it be other than weeds. Thereupon she sketched an urchin in the act of pulling out a tail feather from a parrot. The bird in turn seizes the forelock of the youngster who shows surprise but no resentment at the retaliation. Aptly she designated the charming sketch: "Wie du mir, so ich dir." "As you to me, so I to you."

Her love for anything that lived and fluttered, this genuine Franciscan trait, had marked Sister Innocentia even as a young child. Her loved ones tell of her distress when she saw a fly caught fast on a sticky paper. Tenderly and carefully she would free it from its plight, wash the stickiness from the tiny legs and wings, and put the creature in the sun to dry. Joyfully she would clap her hands as the tiny thing flew away, to be secretly swatted by Lisi or one of the other members. This love for God's creatures she later manifested in a special way toward children. And this trait of character stood her in good stead in dealing with them. She knew how to win even the most shy and reluctant. Children who had never seen a nun, would involuntarily respond to her gentle winsomeness. She would play with the timid and bashful, tell them stories, put colored crayon into their hands and urge them to draw. There was never a dull moment in her art classes. Even the youngest learned and her keen eye readily detected the least talent for her loved art. Usually her little scholars were so absorbed in their droll creations, that it was a joy and delight to the heart of Sister Innocentia to watch their feeble attempts. And this observation was not without its own reward. Sketches by the dozen of these budding artists graced the studio of Sister Innocentia as she furtively sketched the tiny enthusiasts.

Little Zita, a neighbor's child, accosted Sister Innocentia: "Please, sketch me, Sister." At an assuring smile from the Sister, the little one crept closer and whispered: "Will you draw me with my Sunday shoes on?" "Put on your prettiest Sunday shoes," was the gracious response. What was the chagrin of this tiny daughter of Eve, when on calling for her picture, she discovered that the amused artist had sketched only the vain little head.

The late confessor Bishop Johann Sproll, who had suffered tortures under the Nazi regime was also a target for her ready wit. The bishop had a lively interest for her work and loved to visit her studio. On one occasion he remarked: "When I come again, I will bring a comb so that you can groom your children better." Sister Innocentia nodded smilingly without however letting the implication hamper the freedom of her sketches.

At one time the bishop told her in his gentle persuasive manner of the sufferings and privations of his boyhood. "When I was a boy," he began, "I had always loved study. But this wish could only be gratified at the price of great sacrifice. The distance to the nearest Latin school was five miles. And the five miles I walked to Biberach rain or shine. When it rained I spread my huge umbrella, opened my Grammar and fastened it within the ribs of the umbrella, and studied my Latin and Greek vocabulary in this unique fashion. My umbrella had a huge hole, but that was to advantage, for then I could tell when the rain stopped." Sister Innocentia listened intently to this droll and humorous recital. Perhaps even then there arose in her mind the delightful caricature which might be entitled: "Thus he began, the little great man." She created this sketch for the fiftieth anniversary of his Ordination in 1941 and sent it to him with a humble tribute. His Excellency was so pleased with the picture that he composed the text which now graces the little sketch: "John Baptist Sproll, later attended the Latin School in Biberach. For four years he went daily the distance of fifteen kilometers. When it rained he raised his umbrella and into the ribs fastened his Grammar and thus studied the rules of Greek and Latin Grammar. The umbrella had a hole through which he could see when the rain stopped."

Not even her professors were immune from her innocent pranks. While attending Professor Dasio's classes, she found great delight in catching that interesting personage in some of his characteristic poses. The teacher was loved because of his efficiency and yet feared because of his relentless criticism. To make a perfect copy for Professor Dasio seemed an unattainable goal. Once every week he was wont to collect the anonymous works of his students. His pupils about him, he seated himself in the center of the lecture room,

Courtesy of Sacred Art, New York.

XVIII

Courtesy of Sacred Art, New York.

XIX

Hummel Figures Are Now Sent All Over The World.

Hummel figures manufactured for all over the world

and then taking the papers he scrutinized and criticised each page relentlessly. One day he was so absorbed in this process that he failed to notice Berta, who perched high on a table and flanked on either side by her two allies, who held her paints and brushes, sketched the teacher with zeal and unfeigned devotion. From the resulting sketch she later made a wood-cut upon which she impressed the originality and individuality of this great man in truly masterful and apt fashion. Her first draft she crumpled and threw into the waste-basket. The servant who emptied this receptacle found the sketch and having recognized the professor, he reconditioned the crumpled sheet and then bore it in triumph to Madame Brauneis. She at once recognized the Hummel art and said smilingly: "There is only one who would have dared to do it and succeed so realistically. That is the little rogue of a Hummel." Professor Dasio learned of it and demanded to see the sketch. Without any sign of injured pride at the caricature he remarked: "Tell the rogue she could safely have pulled out the drawer a bit further." The inference was to his lower lip which protruded under any stress or emotion.

An example of Sister Innocentia's impulsive activity and deep piety is furnished by her well-known Sacred Heart Picture. Sister had attended a Lenten sermon. The persuasive and eloquent preacher touched all hearts. But none seemed so deeply moved at contemplating the sufferings of the Savior as was Sister Innocentia. Retiring to her cell, she refused to speak to anyone. Grieving sincerely for the breaking heart of the God-Man she must needs find an outlet for her love and sympathy. Even her meals were forgotten. When she finally appeared, pale and visibly affected, she had found solace and relief in the portrayal of her beautiful and awe-inspiring Savior on the Cross.

No little fame came to Sister Hummel through the

delightful figurines which began to make their appearance in 1934. In Oslau by Coberg in Bavaria on the Thuringian border, stands a large porcelain factory. This vicinity and the bordering French lands have been from time immemorial the center of the German Porcelain Industry. One of the most distinguished propagators of the art is this factory at Oslau, founded in 1871 by Franz Detlef Goebel, the great-grandfather of the present proprietor. Marbles, slates, and slate-pencils for school children were the first products of this firm. Presently coffee cups, milk pitchers, egg cups and children services issued from the growing business. The greater part of this output was destined for foreign trade, especially for America. A decisive improvement came with the introduction of figurines and statues. To this latter art the firm had remained faithful and in comparatively few years the number of employees had reached two hundred. But the business was hard hit financially by prevailing conditions in Europe. Many of the workmen had to be dismissed and the fate of the factory was hanging in the balance.

One day one of the talented factory workers, who thus far had escaped the dread specter of unemployment, was sitting at his desk. Being unoccupied he was paging through the Hummelbuch of Margareta Seeman. Presently he was reproducing some of the cunning sketches in plastic. The Little Wanderer, the Fiddler, and the Chimneysweep stood in neat array before him when the proprietor entered. Scrutinizing the work, he saw their potential value and encouraged the man to finish them. Packing the samples he started on his way for Siessen. Sister Innocentia was adamant. She realized the danger to her art in putting her creations into such forms, but when she saw the beauty of the samples and considered the plea of the proprietor, who told her of the need and distress of the firm, she was ready to discuss the possibility. After long consideration she gave permission for the manufacturing of the Hummel Figurines. Each new figure was brought to her for criticism. Often she would remove a head and replace it otherwise; or with brush in hand, she would soften a shade here or brighten another there.

In consequence of these proceedings, a lively intercourse arose between Siessen and Oslau. At each visit the proprietor would bring with him another workman, so that all might become personally acquainted with the artist. All endeavored to follow the advice and suggestions of the able critic to whom they now owed this new interest and impetus in their work. Presently the sole monopoly for the Hummel Figures was granted to Mr. Goebel. The undertaking grew by strides and today some five hundred and fifty employees are working at the Hummel Figurines.

Friends and admirers of the artist might be interested to know more of the Hummel Figurines. After due selection of fitting models has been made, the artist and sculptor give form to the subject. When the clay model is finished, it is separated into parts and the modeler makes a plaster of paris mold for each separate part. These parts are put together while still a wet mass. The rough figure is now dried and burnt in a kiln at a temperature of 800c. Then the glazing follows and the statue is ready for the painting and the finishing touches. All this labor accounts for the seemingly high price demanded for the products.

In 1936 Sister Innocentia made a personal visit to the factory. Laborers and officials were visibly delighted and pleased with this condescension and they marveled at the modest simplicity of the great artist. For the nun, the pleasure was equally great, for she saw for herself what care and solicitude were placed upon each individual product. One of the sculptors who modeled especially her lyric motifs, told her he preferred to do the most delicate features at his own home, where he could accomplish better results while listening to the strains of the radio music. This the Sister readily understood and she sympathized with the delicate talent of the laborer, for she too was readily affected by her surroundings. At home, in her convent cell, she loved to sing while at work, but only then, when she thought herself alone.

With Sister Laura as companion, Sister Innocentia visited all the departments of the factory giving encouragement and cheer to all and a word of constructive criticism when such was in place. When she was ready to leave, an old man who had been in the service of the factory for fifty years arose, and in the name of all thanked the artist in grateful terms for the assistance which her art was giving to so many who would otherwise be in want because of unemployment. Extremely happy and elated, Sister Innocentia left the establishment, unaware that she was the giver and not the recipient of favors, for the joy which we give to others reflects upon our own souls. God's Benediction rests visibly upon a work which has done so much to spread the mission of joy and love fostered by the humble daughter of Saint Francis.

In the year following her profession, 1935-1936, Sister Innocentia returned to Munich to continue study at the Art Academy. In the fall of 1936, a severe cold forced her to leave the city and return to the Motherhouse at Siessen. She was soon restored to health and worked untiringly at the Convent, making larger models and altar ornaments. The following year she made her final vows, binding herself for life as a Franciscan Religious of the Convent at Siessen.

A second Hummel Book, *Hui, Die Hummel,* appeared in Munich in 1939. This was published by the Ars

Sacra, which company was vying with other companies of Munich to do justice to the Hummel cards.

Sister Hummel had gone a long way during the eight years since her graduation from the Art Academy. But she seemed impelled to be prodigal with her talent and with her physical energy. There was so much to do, so little time in which to do it. She had so much to give—and she did not know that already half of her professional career was spent.

Chapter Seven

THE GREAT CATASTROPHE

OTHER Superior gazed earnestly into the tense faces turned toward her. How much her Sisters had suffered! Could she summon sufficient courage to deal this last blow?

"My Sisters," she began, "it is all over. The government officials are coming to take over our home and we must leave. Go now to your cells and make ready whatever you need. Your loved ones will receive you until the storm subsides. We have been given twenty-four hours to vacate. Those of us who have no other home must find place with those who have. The sick and the old and the feeble must remain here; I will insist on that condition. We will find a corner somewhere. God will not forsake us. Live as good Religious wherever you may go. You will come back. God is good, and we must trust Him. Now, God bless you, my children. Auf's Wiedersehen!"

Mechanically, the nuns dropped to their knees. So much had happened; nothing could surprise them now.

68

They looked pleadingly at their spiritual mother. She understood and raised her hand in maternal blessing.

"May the Lord bless you and keep you.

May He show His Face to you and have mercy on you.

May He turn His Countenance to you and give you peace.

May the Lord bless you!"

Sister Innocentia moved as one in a dream. This peaceful life of the cloister; this living close with God; these blissful days of prayer and work and study—must they all end? She gave one last look at her beloved studio: it was just an ordinary workshop, simple and well-used, but in the past few years its plain walls and scanty furniture had become familiar and dear to her. From the large table near the window she could scan the quiet meadow with its streaks of woodland. Now she must leave it all.

She loved her family and knew she was fortunate to be able to return to her home, but she was unwilling to leave the convent. Her parents welcomed their daughter into their midst although their happiness at having her again was moderated by her own grief at being forced to leave the convent. The Hummel brothers had been called to the service so that the presence of Berta was a comfort to the tried father and mother. She could always continue sketching and painting whether at home or at the Motherhouse.

The Franciscan Sisters of the Siessen Convent, as an educational Congregation, had been gradually despoiled of their rights at the hands of the Nazi party during the years preceding 1940. The dissolution of the folk schools, private and secondary schools, kindergartens and other institutes had meant much suffering and sacrifice for them. The death blow came, however, with the confiscation of the Motherhouse on October 30, 1940. It was then that the nuns were ordered to depart. Within ten days the buildings had to be vacated. All the educational activities were laid low at a single stroke. The students returned to their homes, and only forty of the Sisters were permitted to remain at the Motherhouse. They were confined to a wing of the building that contained the chapel and a few rooms. The remaining two hundred and fifty Religious sought refuge wherever it could be found.

A month later, in December, 1940, twelve hundred German refugees from Roumania were brought to the convent. In the following January the entire farm and convent grounds were confiscated. This act cut off all revenue from the Siessen congregation and the prospects of the Sisters remaining at the convent were very discouraging. It was shortly before this final confiscation that Sister Innocentia asked the permission of her superiors to return to the Motherhouse. There were some among her friends who could not understand Sister Innocentia's eagerness to return to the convent. They even tried to persuade her to leave the convent permanently, give up the idea of religious life, and return to her home to continue a career that promised success. They represented to her that only a straw mat on the floor could be hers as Sister Maria Innocentia, but for Berta Hummel there was assured security, advancement, and fame. Sister Innocentia, however, could make only one choice: to return to the convent even though it meant suffering and privation. She obtained her superiors' permission to return to Siessen where a small sleeping room on the upper floor became her studio for the coming years. There she worked incessantly for the next few years, for she was the main support of the hard pressed community. Although the authorities had not directly forbidden her to continue her work, her pictures could be printed only for the foreign market. Their circulation was not permitted in Germany. In spite of all the inconvenience and interference that she suffered, Sister Innocentia completed two murals for a church in Bavaria, made a series of child pictures, and worked for a publisher who edited her creations in the form of postal cards, and sent them to Switzerland and America.

In the meantime some of the Roumanian refugees quartered at the convent were replaced by Slovenians. The latter were joined in October, 1944, by the French. A life hitherto unknown in the convent precincts now held sway. The few Sisters who remained in the cramped quarters allotted them, spent their time in work and prayer, seeking by their life of sacrifice to obtain grace for their dispersed community. Every day brought fresh anguish in the knowledge of the abuse and injury done to those sections of the convent to which they were denied access—abuses of which they had only a faint hint.

In the autumn of 1944 Sister Innocentia was taken seriously ill with an aggravated condition of pleurisy. She was sent to a sanatorium at Isny and then to Wangen, where it was hoped she would quickly recover. She was, therefore, not living at the Motherhouse when the final day of delivery came.

April 22, 1945, brought the climax for the convent at Siessen. The French took the town without confusion, and already on the following day the community received all its property rights. The occupation forces remained until October 30, 1945, exactly five years from the day on which the Sisters lost possession. The dispersion of the troops was as rapid as it was unexpected. Within twenty-four hours all the occupants quartered at the convent, about one thousand in number, had to leave. The forty nuns, who for five years had lived in cramped quarters in one wing of the building, could take possession of the convent and recall their dispersed Sisters. Suddenly the halls had become still and deserted, and the quiet that the Sisters

71

had missed during the past years returned. The nuns recalled from their various places of refuge, gradually filtered back to the convent grounds to rebuild and restore.

When the superior and her companion made the rounds through the buildings that had been occupied by the refugees, they involuntarily shuddered. Desolation, dejection, and emptiness stared from every hall and room. The worst debris had been removed with shovel and pitchfork, but all seemed chaos and confusion. The shattered windowpanes, the missing latches, the soiled and grimy walls and doors, the ruined floors, appeared beyond recovery. The nuns grimly set to work to repair what they could. Hundreds of buckets of water had to be hoisted from story to story to carry on the work of cleaning and reconditioning. Gradually order came out of the chaos and the building began to resume its former appearance. At times the delay for material, the protracted waiting, made the nuns almost despondent.

With the building somewhat restored, the Sisters' next care was to reassemble the furniture and other property that had been disposed of in order to make room for the crowds sent there by the authorities. The disposition of this property was a blessing in disguise, for kind friends were ready to help on the day of evacuation, and within twenty-four hours most of the chattel and valuables were in the hands of dependable friends. The Sisters had but to reclaim what had been so generously guarded during their enforced exile. When all had been recovered they were cheered by the aspect of the place and gained fresh energy to repair the spiritual and moral damage of the past five years. In February, 1946, they were ready to accept students. At the Mass for the opening of the new semester in the second week of June, the Sisters were joined by civic officials and friends in celebrating the restoration of the school. Dr. Eisele, city counsellor and representative of the French Ministry, and Commissioner of Education Brechenmacher, were present at the opening ceremonies. The chaplain, the Reverend Superior Dietrich, spoke in the name of the Congregation:

"At last the day has come for which we have been praying and yearning. What the Prince of Darkness took from us six years ago, the Holy Spirit has restored to us during these Pentecostal days. Today we again open our Institute. Much of this success is due to the French Ministry which from the very beginning has manifested a keen interest in the convent and its personnel. It is owing to his assistance that the house was evacuated in November and returned to us. Herewith I wish to extend to the Ministry our heartfelt and obligatory thanks."

On that morning Dr. Eisele paid beautiful tribute to the work of the Sisters in his address:

"I had of necessity to be present at this celebration of joy and happiness. May it be granted me to be present on every festal occasion that comes to Siessen. For Siessen is the jewel in my lovely district, the jewel which is treasured by all who know its worth. I rejoice because this jewel will again radiate its pristine splendor, and let us hope, send peace and joy and blessing with its gleam.

"Who can describe the sufferings, tortures, immoralities that these walls have witnessed within these years of exile. No one can realize what labors, tears, and worries, yet what affection and devoted self-sacrificing charity have succeeded in brightening this jewel and transforming this place of desolation into one of peace and contentment. How the mothers must have rejoiced when they read the message of invitation to their daughters! How many a one must have prayed, 'May God be praised! My child will be in good keeping!'

"We need women today with lofty ideals and sublime principles. When our noble sons will have returned from prison, they will bear the scars of war on body and spirit. Only a loving mother and a tender wife can understand and know how to help and heal. In this terrible aftermath of want and despair, who is better able to solace than a loving wife and a tender child? I beg of you, dear Sisters, educate these, your young charges, to the highest ideals. Make of them women on whom one can count to rebuild our loved land and to heal the wounds which the ruthless war has so wantonly dealt. Rear for us good women who will be messengers of joy to all the people and will thereby contribute to the reconstruction of fatherland, Church, family, and Christendom."

Following this encouraging address, the Sisters' choir accompanied by Professor Max Springer, sang the inspiring mystic song of Saint Francis, "The Canticle of the Sun":

"Most high, omnipotent, good Lord,
To Thee be praise and glory, honour and blessing:
Only to Thee, most high, do they belong,
And no man is great enough to speak of Thee.

Be praised, my Lord, with all thy creatures,
And most of all for Monsignor Brother Sun,
Who makes the day for us, and the light,
Fair is he, and radiant, and very splendid:
A semblance, Lord most high, of Thee.

Be praised, my Lord, for Sister Moon and all the stars,
In heaven Thou has made them, precious, bright and
     fair.

Be praised, my Lord, for Brother Wind
And for air and cloud and every weather
By which Thou givest sustenance to all thy creatures.

Be praised, my Lord, for Sister Water,
Useful, humble, precious and chaste.

74

Be praised, my Lord, for Brother Fire
By whom Thou dost light up the night.
Beautiful is he, and joyous, robust, and strong.

Be praised, my Lord, for our mother, Sister Earth
Who doth support and keep us, and produce for us
Her varied fruits and coloured flowers and grass.

Oh, praise and bless my Lord, and thankful be,
And serve Him all, with great humility."

New life had come to Siessen. The staunch courage of the Sisters would renew the strength and influence of the ancient convent. Again, the Siessen that had suffered so many fluctuations in centuries gone by would thrive with life and activity.

Sister Innocentia was not present for the reopening of the school. She had lived at the convent through some of its darkest days, doing what she could by virtue of her talent and prestige, to bridge over the period of need. When she left Siessen for the sanatorium, the convent was probably at its worst period during the second World War. On her return two years later it was beginning a new period, rising from the darkness that had shackled it, but grander in its new freedom and light. She, too, was entering on the period of her greatest triumph and power.

Chapter Eight

LAST ILLNESS AND DEATH

"ON November sixth, 1946, our loved Sister Maria Innocentia went forth to meet Christ. The Lord has given her to us; the Lord has taken her from us; as it has pleased the Lord, so hath it happened. Blessed be His Holy Name."

With those words Mother Superior began her account of the last illness and death of Sister Maria Innocentia Hummel. In the fall of 1944 as we have seen, the artist-nun suffered an attack of pleurisy. Her illness did not seem severe, however, and there was no immediate cause for anxiety. She herself anticipated a speedy recovery and continued to make plans for future works that could be accomplished as soon as her illness passed. On November eighth she was admitted as a patient at Wilhelmstift, a sanatorium for tubercular cases at Isny. She had developed a lung infection in addition to the pleurisy condition. Happy child of Saint Francis that she was, she maintained her optimistic attitude, and far from harboring too great apprehensions for her own health, she was soon carrying on a self-imposed mission of bringing cheer to the other patients.

She admired the work of the Sisters-nurses, Franciscans like herself, but of the convent at Reute. These sisters spent the greater part of the day working in sick-room, laboratory, and treatment room. One day she presented them with a picture she had made in bright colors for their laboratory. She explained that she had made it so that they "might have something more cheerful to look at than X-ray plates and sore spots." Here, too, each Sister's feastday was remembered with an original sketch or greeting card.

Wishing to be left alone as much as charity would allow, she asked to have the simple name, "Maria," on her door. The uninitiated would not know who the occupant was, and she could be left undisturbed to work and pray. She wanted above all to lead the life of a Religious. Then, too, she felt she should do all in her power to get the needed rest and quiet that her condition demanded so that she could quickly recover and resume her usual activity. Her religious life was not a matter of simple routine, but the expression of an inner conviction and an intense spirituality. She tried to bear her cross of illness in the spirit of a true child of Saint Francis, but it was no easy matter for her, young and hopeful of plans and ideas for the future, to lie flat on her back, inactive for weeks. It cost her a great deal, and she had to be brave.

Her love of solitude and recollection, however, did not shut her off from those whom she could help. Near the room of Sister Innocentia was a tubercular patient who was also an artist. She was in a critical condition, but added to her physical malady, was a mental state of despondency bordering on despair. Sister Innocentia showed tender and affectionate sympathy for her and visited her as often as she was able to do so. The example of her beautiful religious life and childlike faith had a strong influence on the woman and was instrumental in bringing about her conversion to the Catholic faith. The nun had the happiness of attending the Baptism and First Holy Communion of her friend, who died shortly after in peace and resignation.

There was only one thing that could exhaust the patience of Sister Innocentia at this time. It was the expression of sympathy and false hopes given by those who had never suffered. It was not difficult for her to detect insincerity, and her candid soul was grieved and disturbed by meaningless pity and promises of a glorious future career by those who could not understand. She was doing all in her power to regain her health and she hoped that the work of which she dreamed could be fulfilled, but she resented the attempt on the part of others to deceive her concerning her real condition.

After five months of rest and special care, Sister Innocentia seemed sufficiently recovered to leave the sanatorium. Secretly, she longed for Siessen, and war conditions being such as they were, she was glad to act on the suggestion that she return to the Motherhouse as soon as her condition permitted. She left Isny on April 11, 1945, but her departure came at a most inopportune time. Isny was soon to be occupied by the French, and already the troops were pouring into the city. This made her trip exceedingly tedious and consequently a greater hardship than it would otherwise have been.

Her restoration to health was short-lived and after a few months she was sent to the sanatorium at Wangen. Her condition was made more critical by dropsy. The editor of the Hummel pictures, a native Swiss, offered to take her to a sanatorium in Switzerland. No passport could be obtained for a Sister companion, and the invalid was reluctant to go alone, so the offer had to be refused. An unexpected relapse followed, and she was brought from Wangen to the Motherhouse in September, 1946. Suddenly her heart began to fail and her mother was summoned. Frau Hummel remained at the convent to assist her dying child. All that medical skill and human love were able to do, failed to save that precious life. Heaven was stormed, but God asked the sacrifice of her young life and the measure of suffering that she willingly gave. On October 11, the feast of the Maternity of Our Blessed Lady, she began to prepare for death. Realizing her precarious condition, she asked for the Last Sacraments. Although she suffered greatly she was resigned and humbly offered her life to God. One day, turning to her parents, she said, "I am happy to go home, but my heart grieves for you."

On the morning of November sixth, Sister Innocentia received Holy Viaticum. Then hour by hour her life flame grew dimmer. The Sisters, prayerful and resigned, surrounded the bed, while she, steeped in the spirit of the Poverello of Assisi, awaited Sister Death. "Oh let me die; I can help you more in eternity."

Then shortly before noon, she opened her eyes and fixed her gaze full of victorious peace and undisturbed calm on an invisible Something. She then looked tenderly and lovingly on her mother. Twelve o'clock struck, and the Angelus sounded from the convent tower. With lighted candle in one hand, rosary and crucifix in the other, Sister Innocentia awaited the arrival of her Spouse. As the Angelus rang and her Sisters and loved ones knelt at the bedside praying this triple salutation to Our Lady, Sister Maria Innocentia departed this life. The words of Mary, "Ecce ancilla Domini," accompanied her into the arms of her heavenly Mother.

The remains were brought to the Convent Chapel dedicated to Saint Mary Magdalen, where, amid a wealth of flowers sent by admiring friends, they awaited interment. Near the beautiful baroque statue of the penitent saint, Sister Innocentia reposed, calm and beautiful, as though in sleep. In spite of the intense suffering of her last hours, her features retained their usual serenity and attractiveness.

The solemn obsequies took place on Saturday, November ninth, at eight o'clock. This was her last entrance into the Convent Chapel which she had loved so dearly and where she had so often kept tryst with her Beloved and had found in His companionship strength and courage for personal sanctification and for blessing on her work. Visitors and friends came to see the remains of the little artist-nun humbly clothed in the habit of the Poverello. After the Requiem Mass, with her parents and Sisters in religion, they accompanied her to the convent cemetery. There row upon row of bronze crosses marked the graves of the Sisters of the Siessen community. A few wooden crosses set apart the newest graves, and Sister Innocentia's was one of these. There her Sisters placed her to await the last resurrection.

Speaking of her to the Sisters who were not present at her death, the Mother Superior summarized her life beautifully:

"With love, zeal, and matured artistic skill she created beautiful works to the glory of God and the edification and joy of His creatures. But one day the good God showed our artist new paths. He took His spouse, ready for sacrifice and privations, still in the joy of her youthful betrothal, into the school of suffering, that He might there imprint His image upon her heart.

"Just as she had reproduced with deep feeling and emotion, the images of Our Lord and His Mother in her art, so now she strove to engrave in her own soul, purified by love and suffering and abandonment to His Divine Will, the Image of Christ.

"The Master called His Bride in the bloom of youth to the eternal nuptials. In a short span she has completed a long life. May she, our blessed dead, behold all that He has prepared for her in the eternal glory. May she also be for us a helper and an intercessor at the throne of God, so that the images of Jesus and Mary may be ever more and more engraved in our souls until the eternal reunion. Pray with us a silent prayer at the grave of our loved one who has left us all too soon."

Sister Innocentia's family and Sisters in religion were not alone in mourning; the secular press, both local and foreign, made note of her death and spoke with regret of the loss that art suffered. In her own diocese of Ratisbon, the *Regensburger Bistumsblatt* of November, 1946, commented:

"Berta Hummel's work developed constantly in breadth and depth. It seems as though the child within her was striving to reach maturity. The fact that her career was cut short just at a time when one was expecting greater things from her, makes the passing of Sister Hummel more distressing. Man's work is the result of his inner self and of his personality. The works of Sister Hummel had such a strong and genuine appeal because behind them there was a personality which was striving after final perfection. Art gave her the means for the expression of surrender to the Eternal Beauty, God, and it was at the same time, the emanation of an all-embracing love for man to whom she longed to give a complete share in the riches of her inner self.

"Those who were acquainted with the artist were not surprised that she was unwilling to remain in the world, for they saw in this decision the outburst of an inner striving, an impulse to leave the world and give herself wholly to God in religion in order that she might enrich the world with the fulness of her religious experience.

"She who has left this earth so prematurely will continue to endow us in the future, by her creations which she has left for our joy and edification, and which will continue to grow in popularity. From her early death, which she, with beautiful Christian self-surrender, welcomed with a happy smile that one finds in her child pictures, there goes forth perhaps a greater force than that which emanates from her precious creations—a force that sends comfort and strength into a time filled with sorrow and sacrifice."

Chapter Nine

THE ART OF SISTER INNOCENTIA

*I*N speaking of Sister Innocentia after her death, her superiors at Siessen summarized her work in these words:

"Sister Innocentia considered it her sacred mission to give and foster joy through her art. Her constant aim had been to give joy to others; for this she labored daily among her Sisters. She desired to carry joy into the sorrowful hearts of men. She never coveted fame. Her only ambitions were to be an apostle of joy, an angel of peace, a missionary for Christ, and a true child of her heavenly Mother."

The statement that Sister Innocentia fostered joy through her art is probably the keynote in the interpretation of her work and message. She was gifted with the unusual prerogative of delving deeply into the heart of things, of finding the Creator in His creatures and reproducing Him in her models. For that reason she found beauty and joy in all that she handled or depicted.

Her pictures and figurines make one happy; they fill one with a certain spiritual satisfaction. From her creations one can learn to appreciate the simple ordinary things of life, and convert them to spiritual assets. The world needed the perception of Sister Innocentia's work to be helped to see the beauty inherent in the simple and commonplace. Her apparently ordinary pictures, original and individual as they are, warm the heart and produce an inner joy that often cannot be evoked by themes more sublime. In her secular subjects, she seldom selects the lofty or the profound. It is the everyday event, the ordinary person, the trivial item which others usually pass over in contempt, that Sister Innocentia picks up, studies carefully, and then reveals in all its beauty and meaning through a few deft strokes of her brush. She makes no attempt to portray social or spiritual problems; she does not pose as a moralist. She simply points out what joy and humor can be derived from the drab and the inconsequential.

Sister Innocentia is, above all, the artist of childhood. Her children's pictures established her reputation, and although her work was not confined to this field nor limited by it, her greatest popularity probably arose and will continue through the appeal of her children's pictures. She has studied these little ones and caught them in every phase of life. They are playful, happy, carefree youngsters, clad in patched clothes, worn stockings, and quaint immense shoes. They are all true to life, for Sister Innocentia took them out of her surroundings, having caught them in those charming, winsome moments that are so fleeting, yet so alluring.

Included in some of the children's pictures are caricatures that demonstrate Sister Innocentia's keen sense of humor. There are others besides the very young that she depicts thus for one's amusement. The mild satire in these caricatures is not incompatible with the deep sincerity and thorough penetration of her more serious subjects, even the religious. She paints little people and old folks as they look in their best moments, then places them in situations that are ludicrous or that bring a humorous reaction, compelling one to laugh or merely to smile, more often to chuckle. Most of her secular creations, particularly the humorous, do not merely show a picture. They tell a story, tragically comic at times—as when the five-year-old attempts to scale the fence in his franctic efforts to escape the dread monster of a frog that has come unbidden as his playfellow. But although they are sometimes seen in ridiculous situations, they are all happy mortals, roguish but innocent, sufficient but never sophisticated.

Only a cursory glance through the scores of Hummel creations, both religious and secular, will reveal the artist's love and appreciation of nature. In this she reflected most faithfully the ideals and temperament of the Franciscan tradition. Even as a child, Berta liked to sketch the flowers, the birds, the trees, any and all of God's creatures. The Poor Man of Assisi captured these little things of God in his song; the little Hummel of Massing caught them on her brush and held them fast. There is little wonder that she was attracted to don the habit and adopt the rule of life of the Poverello who lived so close to nature. She was a true child of Saint Francis in her ability to divine the presence of the Creator in the humblest and least of His creatures. Some would say that she showed partiality for the bee, since her own patronymic signified "the bumble." While the bee is conspicuous in some of her secular pictures, it is by no means inevitably present.

It would be rank injustice to place Sister Innocentia's religious pictures in the background. Had she not produced any of her child pictures, she would still be unique in her sacred art. Her Infants, her Madonnas, and her Saints show deep piety and religious fervor. A striking proof of the effect produced by only one religious creation can be obtained from the account of Marga Thome, who had occasion to come in contact with Sister Innocentia's "Infant of Krumbad" during a critical period of her life.

The Infant of Krumbad was made by the artist after she had become a Religious. Sister Maria Innocentia visited the Sanatorium of Krumbad as companion to the Mother General who was a guest-patient. The institution is conducted by the Sisters of Saint Joseph of Ursberg. While there, her superior saw how much everyone loved a picture Sister Innocentia had made of the Infant Jesus, called by her "The Slumbering God." She acceded to Sister's request to make an Image for the Christmas Crib at Krumbad. After she left the sanatorium Sister Innocentia set to work and when Christmas came the beautiful Infant arrived at Krumbad to become the treasure of the institution. Marga Thome described her own reactions on seeing this Infant for the first time:

"Christmas 1939—a Christmas never to be forgotten, a Christmas spent, not with Berta Hummel personally, but beside the crib whose Infant had been modeled by that famous artist.

"Evacuated from a city of western Germany, exiled and homeless, we found refuge at Krumbad, in the convent of the Bavarian Sisters of St. Joseph. The Sister Superior told me, on Christmas Eve, that the Christchild which we were about to behold in the chapel crib had been made by Berta Hummel; that Sister Innocentia—the name of this artist as a Religious—had spent a short time in this very convent and had sent this precious gift to Krumbad after returning to her own community.

"I had always been a great admirer of Berta Hummel's art. I loved the armies of jolly, carefree, innocent little boys and girls whom she had sent out into the world, whose charm had captivated the hearts of young and old. I doubt if there had been a painting of hers of which I did not have a copy among my cherished treasures, but I could no longer call even one of those lovely things my own. Yet, it was Christmas; I longed for the coming of the Christchild, and anxiously waited to see the little Infant modeled by the beloved artist, the only one of its kind ever created by her skillful fingers.

"Finally we were summoned to assist at the Midnight Mass. The chapel was beautifully decorated, the crib surrounded by an exquisite array of red and white blossoms, products of the Sisters' love and skill; candles, scarcely available anywhere, flickered among the blossoms and added to the spell of the hour and place. In the crib lay the figure of Him, Who was and is our One and All. Oh, this Infant, so sweet, so small, so very, very poor! A Child, Who took upon Himself our sins, our misery, our poverty, our privations, our humanity. Here was a Child before Whom we could bend our knees and proclaim: 'Et incarnatus est.'

"How marvelously Sister Innocentia had succeeded in expressing her profound admiration for the heavenly Child and what she had wanted to say: 'Behold the extent of His love.' A wonderful consolation, peace and joy emanated from this poor Child in the crib. Here the restless longing for home was satisfied; here our lamentations ceased; sorrow was turned into resignation, yes, even into joy. Here was true rest; I felt at home. Here I realized His love which had shared everything with us. Never before had the 'Et incarnatus est' become such a living reality for me as in this hour, before this crib. Never before had the angels' words, re-echoing from the Sisters' choir, 'Behold I bring you tidings of great joy,' filled my heart with such heavenly peace and gladness.

"In my heart I thanked Sister Innocentia. How beautiful and well-chosen that name appeared to me in this hallowed hour! I thanked her for the message of this Christmas, and I still give thanks to her for the grace and send greetings of love into her eternal Christmas.

"At that time—Christmas 1939—she was still separated for a few years from that everlasting Christmas. Perhaps she had had some foreboding of the sufferings and humiliations that were to come upon her land, upon herself, upon all of us. Perhaps this had urged her to form this touchingly poor, sweet Infant and put it before us as our only salvation, our only consolation, our only happiness.

"On that same Christmas, 1939, more joy came to me through Berta Hummel. After Midnight Mass, returning to my room I found a tiny, sparkling Christmas tree on my table, put there by loving hands; and under it I discovered among other lovely presents, a complete set of Berta Hummel's Christmas pictures. How happy this precious gift made me. I spread them out, all of them, and felt as if my belongings had in part been restored to me.

"There they were, those darling little people, from the land of happy childhood. They were so carefree, so jolly; no deceit, no political intrigue marked the innocence of their childlike gaiety. Their attire was so simple; they seemed so little concerned about fashions, so natural and real in appearance and action. But how attractive they were in their durable little pants and skirts, their big heavy shoes or, maybe, lacking one shoe or stocking; with hair loosely hanging about their heads or in thick braids, standing stiffly off from chubby little faces. And they were oh, so amusing to look

88

at! Their smiling countenances were greeted everywhere with laughter and created genuine good will.

"One little boy attracted my attention in particular. He was peeping through a hole in the garden fence and grinned at us so happily that I felt as if a sunbeam would shine into my very soul. More charming than the birds, flowers, and butterflies surrounding the little fellow was his darling smiling face. Only a genuine artist could give to the world a smile like this. How true to life also was the picture of a youngster perched high upon the garden wall, at a safe distance from the little frog at which he stared in terror, yelling and screaming for help. How well maternal instinct and solicitude were portrayed in the little tot washing her doll and its attire so tenderly, her own precious self all dripping and exhausted from the ordeal. There was also the little culprit sitting in the corner and gazing in despair at the menacing bundle of switches. His expression said plainly, 'I just don't understand the world anymore!' But a little black kitten pressed close to him as if to say, "What's the matter with you, my jolly playmate? What have they done to you?'

"Before me was a series of laughing little ones under a huge umbrella: Hansel and Gretel, Lucky Hans, the Adventurous Traveler with his bag as well as his parasol.

"How I cherished these unique pictures, especially on that dramatic day! Who could draw a better picture of the little Savior wrapped up like a Bambino? Here was a true Victim, a symbol of total surrender. More often she depicted the Christchild surrounded by the children of men—children of every race, every land. They were, where they ought to be, at the Crib of the dearest of children.

"Amid these guileless, happy people I felt the joy and peace of Berta Hummel's noble soul radiating from her paintings. The artist had become a missionary of joy, a fitting instrument in the hands of the Divine Artist. She had sent those carefree creatures out into the world and wherever they went, they found a hearty welcome. They, in turn, taught men to laugh again, to become, at least for a time, children once more, forgetting cares and worries. They traveled everywhere, no boundaries hindered their advance; they visited young and old, rich and poor, the learned and the illiterate. And everywhere arms opened wide to receive them; and everywhere was heard a pleading voice: 'Oh, come all ye children!' It was a pilgrimage of joy and I kept repeating: 'Dear Sister Innocentia, I thank you!' "

While the Infant of Krumbad is the only work of its kind in sacred art from the hand of Sister Innocentia, religious subjects were not neglected in her pictures. Her sacred themes are manifold. Her Madonnas are the acme of all that is untainted, innocent, humble, profound. They are as original and individual as are her other subjects. Religious themes of her larger works are not nearly so well known as are her earlier creations which have become popularized through reproduction on Christmas and other holiday cards.

The work of Berta Hummel, like that of every outstanding craftsman, has called forth comment and criticism. There are those who see paradox in her reconciliation of the devotional and the ludicrous; others are quick to acknowledge the tremendous output of her facile brush and pen, and the wide range of her interest. None can deny her popularity and her ability to give pleasure. Her art does not need profound study; its message is obvious, and it is always pleasing. Agnese Dunn has called her "Germany's good-will emissary," and little consideration is needed to recognize the appropriateness of this designation. At the time when her work was ostracized by the Party as contradictory to the concept of the superman of the

Third Reich, when she herself was exiled as a nun and a useless member of the state, the little fair, blue-eyed nun was making a staggering conquest of hearts in lands outside the fatherland. With the little children of her pictures, with the cunning old women, and chuckling or puzzled old men she established her place in every country where her work penetrated. Though she hid herself in a cloister, her eyes, her hands, her heart lost none of their power; though she entrenched herself behind convent walls, she went forth to conquer ever new and varied worlds. An insight into the perennial influence of Berta Hummel was well perceived by Marga Thome who succinctly estimated the artist's work:

"Berta Hummel left us at an early age. She has gone, but the children of her art live on. May they continue their march through this world of tears, carrying true and real joy into the hearts of men."

Epilogue

KNOW YOUR HUMMELS

ONE of the outstanding features of the Leipzig Fair held in the spring of 1937, was an array of figurines depicting children in quaint and attractive poses. The little statues were exquisitely modeled and so true to life that they attracted universal attention. Inquiring purchasers learned that the originals were the work of a young nun of remarkable artistic ability who had studied children in every phase of life. A porcelain factory in Thuringia was making these plastics, but the price plus the tariff made their sale outside of Germany almost prohibitive. One firm, Schmid Brothers of Boston, would not be deterred from investing in these unique ceramics. They found out soon after sale began in the United States that they could not keep up with the demand. The little Hummels had made their solemn entry into America; they had captured eyes and hearts and were destined to be popular.

When war began in September, 1939, no more goods could be received from Germany. At this time Sister

Innocentia was still supervising the reproductions, modeling and correcting the finished products both at the convent and in the factory. The income from the figurines, half of which went to the state during the Nazi regime, was practically the sole means of support for the Siessen Convent during the war. The continued demand for the statues in the United States led to the manufacture of substitutes which were far from satisfactory owing to the lack of development of the ceramic industry. Presently imitations of the figurines began to appear in every shape and form. Clumsy substitutes resulted in loss to the manufacturer until finally, Ars Sacra of New York, the sole distributors of the genuine Hummel Prints in America, produced an imitation of comparative excellence. Made of composition, the American product is heavier than the imported.

To collectors throughout the world and to all lovers of children the figurines of little boys and girls are synonymous with Hummel. There have consequently arisen so many imitations that one must know the Hummels in order to distinguish them. According to the artist's mother, the fact that so many imitations began to appear in the United States, China, and elsewhere, vouches for the popularity of the Hummels. With the occupation of southern Germany by the United States forces, the little statues are again coming into their own. Through the office of the Military Government of Germany, Berta Hummel's figurines are crossing the ocean to refresh and amuse the American public. Sister Maria Innocentia's royalties still continue to support the members of her convent at Siessen and enable them to extend their charitable works.

In July, 1947, Schmid Brothers of Boston announced:

93

"We are the sole distributors of the original Hummel figurines which are made in Germany by a factory that has the exclusive contract with the religious Order of which Sister Hummel was a member. A royalty is paid to the Order for every figurine that is sold. These genuine Hummels can be readily distinguished from reproductions and imitations by the name Hummel which is inscribed in the plastic."